Intimate Affairs

Spirituality and Sexuality in Perspective

❏ ❏ ❏

edited by
Martyn Percy

DARTON · LONGMAN + TODD

First published in 1997 by
Darton, Longman and Todd Ltd
1 Spencer Court
140–142 Wandsworth High Street
London SW18 4JJ

© 1997 Martyn Percy

ISBN 0–232–52207–3   20024655

A catalogue record for this book is available
from the British Library

Thanks are due to the following for permission to quote
copyright material: Chatto and Windus and the Estate of Norman
MacCaig for extract from 'Between Mountain and Sea' from *Voice
Over* by Norman MacCaig; Faber and Faber Ltd for extract from
'September 1, 1939' from *Poems, Essays and Dramatic Writings
1927–1939* by W H Auden; Janet Morley for 'Hymn to Wisdom';
Wild Goose Publications/The Iona Community, Glasgow, for
extract from *The Iona Community Worship Book*.

Unless otherwise stated, the biblical references in this book
are taken from the New Jerusalem Bible, published
and copyright 1985 by Darton, Longman and Todd Ltd
and Doubleday & Co. Inc.

Designed by Sandie Boccacci
Phototypeset in $10^{1}/_{2}/14^{1}/_{2}$pt Palatino by Intype
Printed and bound in Great Britain by
Redwood Books, Trowbridge, Wiltshire

Contents

□ □ □

Contents

The Contributors

◻ ◻ ◻

Revd Dr Martyn Percy is Chaplain and Director of Theology and Religious Studies, Christ's College, Cambridge.

The Rt Revd Dr Rowan Williams, formerly Lady Margaret Professor of Divinity at Oxford, is now Bishop of Monmouth and associate lecturer at Bristol University.

Dr Grace Jantzen was lecturer at King's College, London, and is now Professional Research Fellow at Manchester University. She gratefully acknowledges the financial support of the John Rylands Institute.

Angela Tilby is a theologian, broadcaster and commentator on religious affairs. She is currently preparing for ordained ministry in the Church of England.

Dr Margie Tolstoy is a member of Darwin College, Cambridge, and a Research Fellow for the Institute for Religion and Society in Contemporary Europe.

Dr Elizabeth Stuart is the compiler of *Daring to Speak Love's Name*, and is a lecturer at the University of Glamorgan.

The Contributors

Dr Anthony Dyson is Professor of Theology at the University of Manchester.

Dr Mary Grey is Professor of Theology at La Sainte Union College, Southampton University.

Acknowledgements

□ □ □

There are many people to mention in connection with the genesis of this book. Besides the preachers who came to Christ's College, Cambridge, in the Lent term of 1996 to deliver these lectures as sermons, I wish to thank two Masters and the Fellows of the College for their warm support. Professor Sir Hans Kornberg FRS encouraged the series originally, before leaving his posts in Cambridge to work in Boston, Massachusetts. Dr Alan Munro, his successor, also supported the programme of sermons. The students at the College – for whom the series was mainly intended – proved to be both enthusiastic and critically engaged with the material, which of itself had an enormous value. Sarah Jones of the Cambridge Arts Cinema has also been most helpful in discussions about the contents. On a personal note, I have benefitted in the past from the hospitality of a local LGCM group, whose warmth, brokenness, courage and spirituality often touched me deeply. Indeed, I have often been encouraged by friendships and conversations with those who are prepared to stand between tradition and truth, dogmatism and experience, respecting and working with both. Real spirituality is not often born on mountain tops, nor learnt on the sea of faith, but arises when people discover themselves in the God who came to earth in flesh, and is still engaged with that life. My parents, Roy and Sylvia, have taught me many things about love, not least its power to bind people together, ameliorate them in relationships and then create new ones through friendship and openness. As always, my wife, Emma, has encouraged, supported and mollified me, helping me to gain new perspectives by simply being herself. To her, our children (Benjamin and Joseph), I gladly dedicate this book.

Honey and salt – land smell and sea smell
as in the long ago, as in forever.

The days pick me up and carry me off,
half child, half prisoner,

on their journey that I'll share
for a while.

They wound me and bless me
with strange gifts:

the salt of absence
the honey of memory.

Norman MacCaig, 'Between Mountain and Sea'
from *Voice Over* (Chatto & Windus, 1988).

Martyn Percy, Cambridge, 1996

Intimate Affairs

Introduction

Spirituality and Sexuality in Perspective

❏ ❏ ❏

Martyn Percy

This book began life as a series of sermons based on film titles, each one of which offered a perspective on an area of sexuality. It will be obvious to many readers that the Church has often struggled in the past with issues of sexuality, and will no doubt continue to do so. Similarly, the world of cinema has often struggled with portrayals of sexuality: censorship, the law courts and public opinion have all had their part to play in the past, and will probably do so in the future. The idea of linking films to sermons about sexuality may seem curious at first, but there are a number of reasons for the alliance.

First, the cinema and ideas about sexuality share a history of censorship, development and tolerance in this century. There is a sense in which the two mirror each other. That attitudes to sex have changed this century there can be no doubt. Cinema has recorded these shifts in perspective, often unconsciously, but sometimes critically too. Equally, our moral horizons are generally broader in the late modernist and post-modern world, which also requires some re-evaluation. Second, many people derive some knowledge about sexuality through television or film: drama and story teach and influence us more about ourselves than many would like to admit. Portrayals of sexual activity are certainly more 'fleshy' than they used to be: but are they 'realistic', or are they 'idealised' encounters? And what kind of constraints does that place on viewers? Furthermore, what about male and female role-models in films: how 'true' are they, and to whom? Third, it felt appropriate to bring the texts of Scripture alongside contemporary life, including its fictional forms, to see how the Bible might speak afresh to issues of sexuality. In other words, there is a ternary relationship between the preacher, the Bible and contemporary culture: self, Scripture and society together in dialogue. The reason for this strategy is simple. Whenever there is a debate about sexuality in the Church, there are often predictable forms of argument that quickly polarise the discussion, rendering any agreement or lack of it rather stale. In using film and the Bible together, I have worked with a presupposition that both share a fundamental task: namely, at their best they help society reflect on its identity and values, but in such a way as to enable it to transcend itself, and discover deeper truths. In a way, this is the task of 'broadcasting', and I am a firm believer in Christian tradition engaging with this vision, rather than its opposite, namely 'narrowcasting' – reducing horizons of reflection in order to control behaviour either because of or through fear.

Because of my trust in this vision, I quite deliberately adopted a balance in the plurality of voices chosen to speak. There is a mixture of men and women. Although we all share a common faith in Jesus Christ, different denominations are represented: Anglican, Roman Catholic and Free Church. Our sexualities are different too, in order that a one-sided perspective might be avoided. However, we are united in our desire to explore sexuality and spirituality in a way that makes sense in contemporary society, yet is not uncritical of it either, since we are rooted in a faith in God that is constantly embarking on a new culture – the Kingdom of God. In this sense, I suppose you could say that we are offering a type of 'directional plurality' here; a faithful guidebook rather than a rulebook, creativity rather than a manual.

You will doubtless be wondering why I chose certain films as titles for sermons, and if the essays will now make sense to you, even if you have never seen the films in question. Let me try to allay your fears. Each film title is used by each author as a 'peg' for an issue, so a knowledge of the film itself is not *essential*. For example, if there had been a chapter about homosexuality and the clergy, it would not have been necessary to have seen the film *Priest* (1995) to appreciate the nuances of the discussion. My choice of film titles therefore reflects the issues to be discussed in relation to sexuality, and the Bible passages chosen reflect the dialogue with spirituality. In one or two cases, this debate has become quite rich. The Bible texts included at the beginning of each essay are those used as readings for the Evensong services which provided the original context for the sermon series. The third reading was the Psalm for the evening, which was sung: it was not necessarily directly relevant to the subject and therefore has not been given in full.

And so to the films and topics themselves. *The Graduate* (1967) was a landmark in exploring sexual licence in the 1960s, yet even here – if you look carefully

– Dustin Hoffman wears his underpants in bed with his mother's best friend, Mrs Robinson. I chose this film to initiate a discussion about sexual revolutions. Written in the 1960s (Calder Willingham and Buck Henry, from the novel by Charles Webb), the behaviour of the characters typifies the public awareness of the changing nature of sexual relations. Ironically, although 'scandalous', it is a curiously moral film. *Forbidden Fruit* (1922) starred 'naughty' Agnes Ayres in one of the first films by Cecil B. de Mille to address a number of taboo subjects in relation to sex. In his essay, Rowan Williams uses the concept of forbidden fruit to explore sexual ethics in the New Testament. Any discussion about AIDS/HIV could borrow from a number of films, the most obvious being *Philadelphia* (1994). But I chose *Peter's Friends* (1992) because of the student reunion angle: it is a straightforward story about a man who invites his friends for a houseparty in order to say 'goodbye' to them: he is HIV positive. With characteristic style, Grace Jantzen challenges notions of shame and guilt, and invites us to ponder a more holistic and healing concept of 'pride'. *When Harry Met Sally* (1989), aside from the memorable scene in a restaurant ('I'll have what she's having . . .'), is set over a twelve-year period, asking whether there can be friendship between men and women without sex. Angela Tilby, in an essay some might have been tempted to read already, explores the mystique of orgasm in relation to spirituality, drawing on Scripture and mystical traditions.

Pornography would usually be seen as an abuse of sexuality. Yet as Margie Tolstoy points out, there are deeper power and gender issues at work in graphic portrayals of sexuality. *Blow Up* (1966) is Michaelangelo

Antonioni's hedonistic, frank treatment of sex and nudity, and is still rarely seen in the USA. Given that pornography is often exaggeration, this seemed like a good title! *A Walk on the Wild Side* (1962) achieved cinematic distinction for its subtle, novel treatment of lesbianism. Elizabeth Stuart is already well-known for her distinguished work on theologies of friendship and gay issues, and her essay is a carefully nuanced argument against homophobia. The last two essays are about spirituality and being – male and female. When faced with deciding what film to use to reflect on male sexuality, I chose *Carnal Knowledge* (1974), which provoked a Supreme Court ruling against it for its handling of Jack Nicholson's ultimately sated sexual adventures. Nicholson functions as an alter-ego here; his maleness is a popular caricature. This choice was not meant to preempt the outcome of Anthony Dyson's work, which is most intriguing in its treatment of masculinity. Almost the last word has gone to Mary Grey, the feminist and Catholic theologian. No book about sexuality would be complete without a treatment of feminism and sexism, and the 'icon' of Marilyn Monroe seemed a perfect foil. *All about Eve* (1950) had much of its original language censored; however, nobody thought to censor Marilyn Monroe's character being treated like a theatre critic's 'plaything' in the film.

There is a final essay, a kind of addendum to the sermon series that looks at some of the issues I think may be important for the future. There are also some tables which may provoke more thought, suggestions for further reading and a concordance that might enable the book to be used practically as a primer for personal use, group discussion or seminars. Whatever your

5

perspective on sexuality and spirituality, it is my hope, along with the authors, that the essays here will *begin* a process of reflection rather than terminating one. All of us have much to learn in the field of sexuality and spirituality, and this book is just one more signpost along the road that may allow Christians of differing persuasions to come together and be. To truly be the Church, the body of Christ, the social form of the Truth, in which we all have a place where 'we can see face to face' (1 Corinthians 13:12).

The Graduate

Sex and the Sexual Revolution

❏ ❏ ❏

Martyn Percy

Genesis 2:18–25

Yahweh God said, 'It is not right that the man should be alone. I shall make him a helper.' So from the soil Yahweh God fashioned all the wild animals and all the birds of heaven. These he brought to the man to see what he would call them; each one was to bear the name the man would give it. The man gave names to all the cattle, all the birds of heaven and all the wild animals. But no helper suitable for the man was found for him. Then, Yahweh God made the man fall into a deep sleep. And, while he was asleep, he took one of his ribs and closed the flesh up again forthwith. Yahweh God fashioned the rib he had taken from the man into a woman, and brought her to the man. And the man said:

> This one at last is bone of my bones
> and flesh of my flesh!
> She is to be called Woman,
> because she was taken from Man.

This is why a man leaves his father and mother and becomes attached to his wife, and they become one flesh.

Now, both of them were naked, the man and his wife, but they felt no shame before each other.

1 Corinthians 13
Though I command languages both human and angelic – if I speak without love, I am no more than a gong booming or a cymbal clashing. And though I have the power of prophecy, to penetrate all mysteries and knowledge, and though I have all the faith necessary to move mountains – if I am without love, I am nothing. Though I should give away to the poor all that I possess, and even give up my body to be burned – if I am without love, it will do me no good whatever.

Love is always patient and kind; love is never jealous; love is not boastful or conceited, it is never rude and never seeks its own advantage, it does not take offence or store up grievances. Love does not rejoice at wrongdoing, but finds its joy in the truth. It is always ready to make allowances, to trust, to hope and to endure whatever comes.

Love never comes to an end. But if there are prophecies, they will be done away with; if tongues, they will fall silent; and if knowledge, it will be done away with. For we know only imperfectly, and we prophesy imperfectly; but once perfection comes, all imperfect things will be done away with. When I was a child, I used to talk like a child, and see things as a child does, and think like a child; but now that I have become an adult, I have finished with all childish ways. Now we see only reflections in a mirror, mere riddles, but then we shall be seeing face to face. Now, I can know only imperfectly; but then I shall know just as fully as I am myself known.

As it is these remain: faith, hope and love, the three of them; and the greatest of them is love.

The Graduate

Psalm 25:1–10

A broad-minded vicar was once invited by an equally broad-minded headmistress to talk to her sixth form about Christianity and sex. The vicar's wife usually kept his diary for him, and being a rather prudish woman, the vicar entered the engagement in his diary as 'talk to girls about sailing'. He duly went to the school, and delivered what turned out to be an enlightening and absorbing lecture. A day or so after the talk, the headmistress encountered the vicar's wife. 'Your husband was marvellous the other day,' exclaimed the headmistress, 'he was so helpful in his approach.' The vicar's wife looked puzzled. 'I can't imagine what he knows about the subject,' she replied, 'he's only done it twice and the first time he was sick and on the second occasion his hat blew off.'

When religion and sex are mentioned together, there is nearly always a predictable range of responses: from embarrassment to posturing, from sensationalism to exasperation – the topic seldom elicits boredom. Traditionally, the Church is regarded as a reactionary force when it comes to dealing with sex. The Bible, to some at least, seems to be very unequivocal in its condemnation of certain practices. Homosexuality, lesbianism, adultery are all clearly outlawed. But are they? To others, the Bible seems to be affirmative of contemporary 'social norms': monogamy, a stable family life with little or no sex before marriage, is apparently consecrated in the same texts. But is that right? Still to others, the Bible apparently offers very few reliable patterns for regulating sexual behaviour, because it appears to offer a mish-

9

mash of conflicting and competing ideals. But is that actually correct?

The rules for engaging in this debate tend to travel along well-worn tracks. Conservative Christians tend to pin their hopes on biblical texts and then again on the way in which their Church interprets them. Occasionally, with issues such as abortion, contraception or new technologies for creating human life, the tradition of the Church will suffice as a legislator. Those inclined towards a more liberal disposition tend to try and reason with the same texts and traditions, whilst at the same time attempting to make sense of the present cultural climate. In short, to be more accommodating and open, without necessarily compromising core Christian values.

Each of these strategies risks failure to a certain degree. A preacher who once defended the compatibility of homosexuality and Christianity in a sermon at a Cambridge College was taken to task by some zealous young women after the service. The preacher ignored their complaints completely. When they asked if he could hear them, he replied he could, but that if they had read their Bibles, they would be wearing hats, not be speaking or attempting to teach in church, nor sporting clothes made from mixed fabrics, which are forbidden in the Old Testament. Understandably put out, they further complained that these issues were not essential to Christian belief, but were culturally-bound taboos. You can guess the reply. Anecdotes that are contrary to the liberal tradition and illustrate the contradictions and hypocrisy that sometimes go on are no less common. Proclaiming a gospel of openness and liberation is all very fine, until the stories of abuse and misconduct start to appear on the front pages of the tabloid newspapers. Then questions about the limits of freedom start to surface once again.

Between the liberal and conservative traditions lies a middle way, which many who are religious tend to choose. Generally, it is respectful of texts and traditions, but is also governed by a compassionate heart and a real empathy with all people, recognising that everyone is conditioned and constrained to some extent by our collective cultural baggage. A variety of disciplines and insights have led many to recognise that the history of sexuality itself is a mixed one. For example, attitudes to homosexuality in Western Europe have changed substantially over the past hundred years. The work of psychoanalysts such as Sigmund Freud (*Totem and Taboo*, (1913; New York, Vintage, 1939, etc.) has played a part here, and genetic science is now also showing increasing interest in what drives our sexuality. Are homosexual and heterosexual ways of relating a question of nature or nurture? Can you really claim it is neither, but revelation? And then what of bisexuality, which was familiar to many ancient cultures? Michel Foucault (*The History of Sexuality, Volume 1*, 1976), the controversial French post-structuralist philosopher, adopts a 'language and socialisation' perspective on such issues, arguing that the very structure of our knowledge exerts power over all social objects, including our own human bodies. Medically, the introduction of effective contraception has undoubtedly had an impact on sexual behaviour. Some would say we live in an age of sexual revolution.

These brief observations lead to a couple of fundamental questions. First, has there really been a sexual revolution? If so, what kind of revolution is it, and what are its strengths and weaknesses? Second, why does sex matter? This may sound a rather futile question, but issues of intimacy, knowledge, identity and personhood are all suggested by such questions. Exploring these areas may help to place sex and sexuality in perspective, especially in relation to spirituality, for all those who strive to live and learn in love. Moreover, this is an urgent task, given the contemporary preoccupation with sex, which, underlined by subtle and sublime images, has driven up the thresholds of expectation to dizzying heights. In spite of increased awareness and education, I suspect many feel bewildered and confused by more choices and changes.

So, do we live in an age of sexual revolution? As a parish priest in Bedford, I was often intrigued by the history of the town and the religious life that had been developing over many centuries. It was a great help in understanding the context of ministry in the present. After conversation with a parishioner one day, I was lucky enough to be lent a couple of volumes from the Historical Record Society. One of these volumes (no. 69: *Hundreds, Manors, Parishes and the Church*, 1990) included excerpts from the Archdiaconal visitations of 1578, over four hundred years ago. The report cited the usual problems: structural work not done on churches ('our chansell is in decaye and redye to faule downe, at the default of Trynitye College in Cambridge', p. 175), absent clergy ('we do present that we had no communion but once this yeare...') and people being fined for non-attendance of services. Much more fascinating, however, was the moral record of these parishes. Here was page after page of reports of adultery, illegitimacy, 'whoredom' and general sexual licence ('Adre Cooper was gotten with childe in Turvey by Thomas Parkins...

12

Joans Hewe is suspected to lyve incontynentlye with a wydowe . . . suspicion of whoredom between William Swyngland and John Fletcher's wyfe . . . Barbara Dicons is with child, being not maryd lawfullye'). It is unlikely that there was a minor sexual revolution occurring in Bedfordshire at the time. What the report reflects is the fact that 'immorality' was widespread and public, even if it was not explicitly condoned. Furthermore 'marriage' had a different history in the sixteenth century. Few couples had their union blessed in church; that was a privilege reserved for the wealthy. Most had a simple service at the lych-gate, and given the shortage of priests and their infrequency of visits, couples living together before marriage were not uncommon. The twelve-day festival of Lammas (August) even allowed for 'trial marriages' in some parts of medieval England.

In our own time, we are tempted to visit sexual history through the sanitised eyes of our Victorian forebears: the appeal to a moral or spiritual 'back to basics' ideology rests on this perspective. Yet it is quite patently false, and possibly even dangerous to suggest that there is an unbroken tradition of 'right and proper' sexual behaviour and roles, as though sex was somehow something that was invented in the 1960s. We know from Scripture that there were many different forms of family life expressed in orthodox Judaism. True, monogamy was common, but polygamy and concubines were not unknown, and their offspring were deemed by Jewish law to be legitimate heirs (Genesis 25:6, etc.). The practice of 'betrothal' may well have permitted sexual intercourse before marriage, since proof of fertility and pregnancy might have been an essential prerequisite to getting married. If you had no children, who would care for you in your old age? There were no pensions or residential homes. The lot of barren widows portrayed in the New Testament was consequently a particularly poor one. It is possible that the scandal of Mary's pregnancy is not so much the issue of sex before marriage, as Joseph knowing that he was not the father (Matthew 1:18ff.). Some of this may sound a bit far-fetched, but when you consider the plethora of Christian books that argue the Bible teaches 'old-fashioned family values' such as monogamy, abstinence before marriage, and mothers staying at home and not going to work, it is worth asking 'who is actually proposing a sexual revolution'? Throughout history, women have worked to support their families financially. Nobody minded (poor) mothers being employed: the Victorians had to produce legislation to prevent their children being included in the same workforce! In other words, talk of a 'sexual revolution' may turn out to be a reactionary conservative conspiracy designed to control behaviour and rewrite moral history. Much of what passes for the 'basics' that we are being heralded back to may turn out to be modernist bourgeois Western values, attempting to impose themselves on a post-modern society that has access to many methods of birth control, and is largely free from secular-moral or religious-spiritual control.

Yet contemporary society has a rather ironic attitude to sexuality. The new sexual freedom brings responsibility, which is not always handled well by individuals or society. On one level, society is apparently progressive in terms of the education and advice that are now available. Equally, it can also be exploitative. This need not take the form of degrading or abusive images and practices. The 'myth' or culture of complete sexual fulfilment –

propagated by cinema, television and glossy magazines
– has much to answer for, a theme we shall return to
later. The reactionary reflex that attempts to retreat into
an illusory past in which the grammar of sexual conduct
was clearly defined is comprehensible when one con-
siders the weight of sexual abuse and exploitation. Yet it
also risks exploitation itself, denying rights and freedom
where they are due. The agenda of certain religious cam-
paigners who advocate a return to 'traditional' values
may transpire to be nothing more than a plea for the
sacralisation of selective Victorian middle-class ideals in
society, backed up by a very naïve reading of Scripture,
and little appreciation of social history. Yet it does at
least represent some attempt to stem the tide of moral
confusion, and give guidance where it is needed, as well
as supporting the vulnerable. Perhaps society needs a
series of sexual revolutions, in which practice and values
are constantly re-evaluated in relation to justice, truth,
freedom and the rights of individuals and society.

Clearly, sex matters a great deal. The treatment of
sexuality in *The Graduate* (1967) is as good a place as any
to start exploring how and why it actually concerns us.
The film tells the story of a rich Californian ex-student
who is led into an affair with the wife of his father's
best friend, but finally falls in love with her daughter.
Benjamin (the graduate, played by Dustin Hoffman)
presents as an innocent young man who gains a certain
degree of sexual fulfilment through his relationship with
Mrs Robinson. Yet as the film develops, it is clear that
Benjamin finds their personal relationship unfulfilling,
and a more equivocal dependence with Mrs Robinson's
daughter begins to develop. The film concludes with the

new couple eloping, spurred on by the dulcet tones of the Simon and Garfunkel soundtrack.

At face value, the film does not seem to be very moral. Two different kinds of affairs, a lot of deceit and unhappiness, and undertones of a rich and sexual opulence might suggest that there is little in the way of 'good news' in the story. Yet a closer appreciation of the film shows a different side. The obsession with sex as a kind of therapy for Mrs Robinson and as an education for Benjamin is shown to be an inadequate basis for a relationship. The inequality and secrecy of the parties involved suggest that both should find something more appropriate and fulfilling, which Benjamin does in Mrs Robinson's daughter. The film portrays the consequences and exposure of the first affair – quite rightly – as destructive and scandalous, threatening to break apart all relationships and personal identity. But like a kind of resurrection, the new relationship emerges out of the ashes and chaos of the old. Suddenly, the sating of sexual desire is not enough: sex must be a part of wider relational fulfilment. The film ends on a liberating note, showing that a passionate love can triumph over sin, failure and oppression. Quite moral, really.

The early chapters of Genesis provide an allegorical and critical counterbalance for some of these themes. The loss of innocence in the Garden of Eden is indeed catastrophic. Adam and Eve are driven from the garden, and are cursed. Yet there is more to the story than the loss of paradise. Implicit in the text is the suggestion that more knowledge does not necessarily lead to more fulfilment. I am not suggesting here that we cherish ignorance and naïveté for their own sake, because they are somehow blissful and ordained. On the contrary, I am simply repeating a lesson of sexual history, namely that improved knowledge and techniques do not always reflect the state of the heart, and therefore do not always affect relationships in quite the way we might hope. To put this more sharply, sex education does not necessarily make you a better lover. Questions of appropriateness and love need to be addressed, which might lead to a more fulfilling and permanent union. An equally disturbing feature of the Genesis story is the way in which the pursuit of knowledge leads to inequality between the sexes, and division of labour and responsibility. The first two chapters portray an ecology of relational and mutual interdependence, in which 'harmony' is the guiding principle, even though there are many different forms of life. It is selfishness that so often disturbs this equilibrium, and Genesis illustrates the perils of pure self-fulfilment, even if this is disguised by the self-deceit that what is being done is for the sake of another. In Genesis, as in many works of literature and film, the characters involved in the lovers' tryst often learn this only too late, after the fall, and by then the avenues of redemption are often sealed off.

Paul, writing in one of the greatest passages in the New Testament (1 Corinthians 13), offers a deep and systematic expression of what relationships can be if a genuine love is at the heart of government. Interestingly, the pursuit of knowledge and fulfilment is postponed in the passage, reversing the sequence of events in Genesis. Genuine love, we are told, proceeds from belonging, believing and behaving – knowledge comes later. The basis for this is a mutual cleaving, not just between people, but also between God and humanity. The key is *trust*: not so much *what* you know as *how* you know it. It is actually in this activity that true knowledge is gained, where we begin to see God and each other 'face to face'. Knowledge is no longer a cognitive property, but also a matter of the heart, in which giving and receiving constantly enlarges the body of knowledge and the possibilities of love. This is true wisdom. Humanly, sexually and spiritually, all of us learning to pray with Paul: 'Now I know in part; then I shall understand fully, even as I have been fully understood' (v. 12).

Undoubtedly, there are plenty of factors that prevent us from reaching this maturity that Paul describes. The opposite of faith is not doubt but fear, and it is *perfect* love that casts out *all* fear (1 John 4:18). John tells us that there is no fear in love, because 'fear is to do with punishment'. Actually, this places quite a moral burden on the Church and all who aspire to address the relationship between spirituality and sexuality. Clearly, no one loves perfectly, and neither is anyone free from all fear. Yet the deliverance from fear is a highly desirable goal for the Christian if love is to be fostered, and Christians have frequently spent too much time fermenting fear in relation to sex, instead of encouraging a spirit of trust and understanding. I can still vividly remember the apocryphal stories, pamphlets and books that dominated the evangelical youth group I used to attend, and instilled a sense of dread and guilt whenever the subject of sex was raised.

One way of achieving this deliverance from fear might be to talk less of sin, guilt and judgement, and more about *true* fulfilment, stressing the positive aspects of a new sexual revolution that looks forwards rather than backwards. To some extent, this revolution has already begun. It is rare for Churches to stress sex as mainly procreative these days: encouragement of pleasure is implicit in much teaching and preparation for marriage. However, other moral issues remain cloudy. For example, it is easy, on the basis of Scripture, to condemn homosexuality. But how is it 'sinful' if it is practised in a faithful, life-long relationship that is not abusive? Only, it seems to me, in the sense that it might be 'unnatural' or 'disobedient', but given what we now know about theories on the origins of homosexual orientation, this begins to look like a very thin argument.

The task of the Church is to encourage relationships rather than control them, and create the proper context for true fulfilment: every good relationship that is mutual and open to the other(s) is something to celebrate. In turn, this would necessitate being open to the history of sexuality, as well as science and various types of 'therapy', and being honest about the fact that changing patterns of sexuality are fairly constant. History, after all, is the story of change, and no one religious or moral group has the monopoly on 'the basics'. It seems to me that if we do live in an age of sexual revolution at all, it is just an age in which *complete fulfilment* is sought in many things, the obsessions with health and wealth mirroring our absorption with sex. Those who blame 'immorality' on sex education, ignorance or contraception, would do well to remember that the number of pregnancies in England and Wales for the under-sixteen age-group has remained constant at about 6,000 for over thirty years. True there are few live births since the legalisation of abortion, and the consequences of sex (procreation) are no longer necessarily the same. Yet there is still nothing really new about our sexual behaviour. It is just that the post-modern culture demands satisfaction and pleasure for the self at every conceivable level, and imagines that it can achieve this to an extent that might have been envied by our forebears.

So what might the guiding principles for a new sexual revolution be? Clearly, they can still be grounded in Christian traditions and Scriptures. The harmony and equality that Genesis suggests can be emulated, as long as it is understood that the actual pursuit of knowledge is not always a short cut to greater fulfilment. Equally, Paul reminds us that maturity and realism come through the true application of love which leads to wisdom: those who offer or withhold sexual knowledge need to remember their responsibilities to initiate freedom. I fully acknowledge that this 'blueprint' for a new sexual revolution is a risky strategy: the world can abuse a Church that is too open in its morality, as much as it can ignore one that is too closed. The model for praxis, as always, is to look at the love of God poured out in Jesus Christ, and to reflect on the mystery of the incarnation – God becoming vulnerable in human flesh. This is a love that risked rejection and death. A love that affirmed the identity of marginalised and despised individuals by being with them rather than simply rejecting them. Only then did 'sinners' begin to change. A love that had no time for throwing stones or sparring with texts, but simply forgave. Perhaps *The Graduate* does get it right when it proclaims to all those who think that they fall short of God's grace, or to those who are only too ready to condemn: 'Here's to you, Mrs Robinson . . . Jesus loves you more than you can know.'

Forbidden Fruit

New Testament Sexual Ethics

❏ ❏ ❏

Rowan Williams

Genesis 3:1–13
The Fall

Now, the snake was the most subtle of all the wild animals that Yahweh God had made. It asked the woman, 'Did God really say you were not to eat from any of the trees in the garden?' The woman answered the snake, 'We may eat the fruit of the trees in the garden. But of the fruit of the tree in the middle of the garden God said, "You must not eat it, nor touch it, under pain of death."' Then the snake said to the woman, 'No! You will not die! God knows in fact that the day you eat it your eyes will be opened and you will be like gods, knowing good from evil.' The woman saw that the tree was good to eat and pleasing to the eye, and that it was enticing for the wisdom that it could give. So she took some of its fruit and ate it. She also gave some to her husband who was with her, and he ate it. Then the eyes of both of them were opened and they realised that they were naked. So they sewed fig-leaves together to make themselves loin-cloths.

The man and his wife heard the sound of Yahweh God

walking in the garden in the cool of the day, and they hid from Yahweh God among the trees of the garden. But Yahweh God called to the man. 'Where are you?' he asked. 'I heard the sound of you in the garden,' he replied. I was afraid because I was naked, so I hid.' 'Who told you that you were naked?' he asked. 'Have you been eating from the tree I forbade you to eat?' The man replied, 'It was the woman you put with me: she gave me some fruit from the tree, and I ate it.' Then Yahweh God said to the woman, 'Why did you do that?' The woman replied, 'The snake tempted me and I ate.'

John 8:2–11
At daybreak he appeared in the Temple again: and as all the people came to him, he sat down and began to teach them.

The scribes and Pharisees brought a woman along who had been caught committing adultery: and making her stand there in the middle they said to Jesus, 'Master, this woman was caught in the very act of committing adultery, and in the Law Moses has ordered us to stone women of this kind. What have you got to say?' They asked him this as a test, looking for an accusation to use against him. But Jesus bent down and started writing on the ground with his finger. As they persisted with their question, he straightened up and said, 'Let the one among you who is guiltless be the first to throw a stone at her.' Then he bent down and continued writing on the ground. When they heard this they went away one by one, beginning with the eldest, until the last one had gone and Jesus was left alone with the woman, who remained in the middle. Jesus again straightened up and said, 'Woman, where are they? Has no one condemned you?' 'No one, sir,' she replied. 'Neither do I condemn you,' said Jesus. 'Go away, and from this moment sin no more.'

Psalm 97

Perhaps the first thing to say is that there *isn't* really very much in the way of what we should think of as sexual ethics in the New Testament. There are meditations and recommendations to do with marriage, and there are some stark observations about celibacy; there are a few scattered remarks about vaguely defined 'impurity' or 'uncleanness' of behaviour, *porneia*, which seems to refer to anything from adultery to prostitution; there are, in the writings ascribed to St Paul, three disparaging references to sexual activity between men. Jesus is recorded as following a strict line on the admissibility of a man deciding to dissolve his marriage (not exactly a discussion of divorce in the modern sense), and refers in passing to *porneia* as one of the evils that come from the inner core of the self. And that's about it. The overall impression is certainly that sexual activity is an area of moral risk, and that nothing outside marriage is to be commended. But it is, when you look at the texts, surprisingly difficult to find this spelled out in any detail, explored or defended.

Or is it so surprising? We forget easily that the Christian Scriptures were not written to answer *our* questions. We assume that there is an area of human experience called 'sexuality', which is of immense importance, something which needs to be sorted out before anyone can claim to be leading a mature and

23

fulfilled human life. But the world of Jesus and Paul would not have recognised such language. They knew about marriages as a complicated bundle of economic arrangements, ideally involving mutual affection and stability; they knew that young males were most unlikely to resist promptings towards sexual involvement, and generally did their best to stop this damaging excessively the tidiness of arrangements about marriage; they assumed that women were unreliable and easily swayed by emotion, so that they needed protection from casual liaisons, in order to be eligible for a 'good' marriage; they knew about the situation in which an older man took up a younger one, offering him patronage and instruction in return for a modicum of bodily pleasure. They would have been puzzled to see all this brought together under a single heading, or to be asked about their 'sexuality'. There was desire, there were acts of sexual intimacy, there was the important public bond of marriage, indispensable in sorting out issues about property rights and inheritance. They did not need to have much to do with each other.

In a rather odd way, Christianity itself bears some of the responsibility for the emergence of a unified approach to sexual experience and activity – chiefly by giving enormous and increasing importance to sexual abstinence. Early Christians proudly proclaimed their distinctiveness by pointing to the fact that at least a substantial proportion of their number renounced all sexual activity; this was regarded – along with the courage of Christians in the face of death – as one of the proofs of the supernatural power of faith. And inevitably the variety of things renounced – marriage, but also youthful affairs, casual sex with slaves, male or

24

female, and the use of prostitutes – tended to be lumped together as, after all, a single area of human behaviour, and one that was inherently deeply compromising for a person living by faith in Christ and in hope of life everlasting. Despite what a number of silly textbooks and journalistic surveys tell you, the majority of early Christian writers didn't think sex was evil; they simply thought it was too complex for comfort; it weighed you down, tangled your thoughts and emotions unhelpfully, and – well, at the end of the day, wasn't it just a bit . . . undignified? Few of the early Christians sound like neurotics obsessed with the filth of sex (some do); most are simply rather snobbish about it. It's vulgar and messy; best not to bother.

But this is already some way from what the New Testament actually says. For Jesus and Paul, the problem isn't that sex is irrational or vulgar, but that certain kinds of bonding will turn out to be too all-consuming for at least some of the citizens of God's Kingdom. Jesus seems to commend celibacy for 'those who can manage it', particularly those who are called to the life of wandering preachers – the Twelve and their immediate successors. Even there, the rule is obviously not absolute: St Paul mentions in passing that St Peter was accompanied on his travels by his wife. Paul assumes the end of the world is due very shortly: the serious Christian may well feel that being encumbered with a family to provide for might get in the way of what needs doing in the short time left. And Paul evidently doesn't think any other form of sexual union is worth discussing in this context.

What is baffling and sometimes outrageous to the modern reader is just this assumption that, in certain circumstances, sex can't matter all *that* much. And I want to suggest that the most important contribution the New Testament can make to our present understanding of sexuality may be precisely in this unwelcome and rather chilling message. We come to the New Testament eagerly looking for answers, and we meet a blank or quizzical face: why is *that* the all-important problem? Not all human goods are possible all the time, and it would be a disaster to think that there was some experience without which *nothing* else made sense. Only if sexual intimacy is seen as the last hiding-place of real transcendence, to borrow a phrase from the American novelist, Walker Percy, could we assume that it mattered above all else. But we are now in a cultural situation where there really isn't much left of transcendence for a lot of people, and they have to take what they can get. To quote Walker Percy once again, it may be that for more and more people sex is practically the only way they can feel sure they are really *there*, really the object of another's attention. Other cultures didn't and don't share that anxiety: it's really quite important to be reminded of that from time to time, to ask whether having the reassurances of sexual intimacy would be the first priority in times of profound crisis or corporate suffering, whether we'd give it higher priority than attention to pain or to beauty in extreme moments.

All right; but that doesn't help much with the average situation for most of us, where we're not in crisis, not expecting the end of the world and not conscious of a vocation to be a wandering preacher. And what we've just said in fact still presupposes that sex is a very heavily charged, significant matter, if it can in some ways compete, as we know it does, with the claims of other deeply serious areas of our humanity. So let's take as

read the way in which the New Testament comes to us
at an angle from our expectations, and pursue what it
specifically says about what we'd call the sexual in our
experience. Paul is, as always, fearfully unsystematic,
but he hints here and there at a rationale for his somewhat throwaway remarks on marriage and other
matters. His major contribution is I Corinthians 7: if this
had been lost in the post, Christian ethics would have
been very different, since there is more here on sexual
relationships than in all the rest of the New Testament.
Yes, celibacy is a good idea if you can manage it; but
abstinence is hard work, and not a very good idea *within*
marriage. In marriage, says Paul rather startlingly,
neither party any longer owns their own body; it is
given to another. This is ambiguous in its implications,
as several recent commentators have said: 'ownership'
still leaves us with a problem about sex as the exercise
of power, even if it is shared out. But it overturns one
very fundamental assumption of Paul's Jewish and
Greek environment – that the woman has no power
and no independent desire in the married relation. Paul
allows her initiative and responsibility, not only duties;
but the central image is one in which partners *renounce*
the idea that they have rights to be exercised at each
other's expense, and are able to entrust themselves to
the care of another. My *right* is to be honoured, not
coerced, by my partner, but I can only express that by
allowing that my own 'power' in this relationship is
given purely for the purpose of returning the same
honour. Neither is free *from* the other; each is free *for* the
other.

The Letter to the Ephesians, which may or may not
be directly from Paul's hand, makes the connection with

27

the way God in Jesus Christ deals with us: by self-gift and self-sacrifice – though the writer goes on to make a less clear connection between the wife's response of obedience and the Church's obedience to Christ. If we were developing the analogy in terms of what is said in I Corinthians, we might expect some sense that the marriage relation could image Christ's self-gift on *both* sides. But another insight into a possible method for looking at sexual intimacy can be teased out: Christians are meant to reflect the form and style of divine action in all they do; sexual activity is no exception. If God acts for us by letting go of a divine power that is abstract and unilateral and comes in Jesus' life to set us free for working with Jesus and praying with Jesus, this suggests strongly that a sexual partnership that is unequal, that represents power exercised by one person trying to define the other, would fail to be part of an integrated Christian life.

But Paul is speaking only of marriage; does this rule out other kinds of sexual partnership? Paul doesn't say so in quite so many words, but the implication is probably there (and most Christians have read him in this way). Perhaps we might see why such a conclusion could be drawn if we reflect on what he has said about this mutual yielding of power in marriage. All relations are in fact complicated by anxieties and unevennesses in the power and freedom of the partners. Can I trust enough to yield my liberty, to put my power and freedom at someone else's disposal, without covenant and promise, the tangible assurance that my giving is met by another's? Can I take this admittedly great risk without some way of knowing that the other doesn't hold back and reserve their resources just in case I turn out not to be good enough, not to match their fancies or expectations? On the horizon is very definitely the idea that mutual yielding properly goes with mutual promise.

Something of this is also traceable in the last section of I Corinthians 6. Christians don't use prostitutes, because the exploitation of a prostitute involves the whole body of Christ. If I am involved in such a transaction, it affects all the relations in which I am involved as a member of the community of the Spirit. 'Your body is a temple of the Holy Spirit', says Paul; and that Spirit, as he explains again and again elsewhere, is the power by which Christians can live together without rivalry and selfishness, in a climate of mutual giving and receiving. An 'impersonal' sexual transaction poisons the *community's* life; it somehow affects everyone's integrity. So my policy about sexual behaviour isn't just my business: it is part of that vast and often obscure network that gives us our new being as Christians, our being-for-each-other in the Church. The community thus has an interest in what I decide about sex. Not a prurient and gossipy interest; and not that (God forbid) it should be instituting inquisitions into sexual behaviour; but it has a legitimate claim to put before believers their responsibility to the whole body, and thus to ask that sexual commitments be open, a proper public matter, supported by the community and in turn nourishing the life of the community.

These, then, are some of the clues Paul gives. He does not write a rule book, but sets an agenda. Later Christianity thought it better to write rules; it took these insights and set up a wide-ranging and sophisticated scheme of sexual law which eventually turned all this into something rather different. For Paul, the distinc-

tively Christian meanings of sex are shown in relations
of promise and constancy that allow us the freedom to
be vulnerable. If we live our lives otherwise, we hurt
the common life of the Church. But this is not quite the
same as saying categorically that it is only in marriage
that anything of these meanings comes to light, or that
anything other than marriage is sin and nothing else.
I can't see that the New Testament easily allows any
straightforwardly positive evaluation of sexual intimacy
outside a relationship that is publicly committed; but
it does not suggest that the essential test of Christian
orthodoxy lies in a willingness to treat all other relationships as incapable of sharing in the love of God. What
we have is a focal and compelling set of images that can
be translated into terms of behaviour by saying, 'Sexual
intimacy is fully what it should be for Christians, a sign
of God's vulnerable commitment, in *this* context.' Claims
for any other contexts would have to be argued hard –
and the Church has seen no compelling reason for changing its mind about the primacy of 'covenanted'
relationships. The fact that people learn, often by false
starts, by giving and receiving hurts, with the best will
in the world, by discovering their self-deceitfulness and
so on, is another story, a story all too familiar to many
of us; but something of God is discoverable even in what
we may recognise as involving error. In many parts of
the Church, it looks as if the jury is out on the question
of whether some kinds of homosexual relation are effec-
tively of the same kind as the relations between the sexes
that Paul outlines, to the degree that this might outweigh
Paul's denunciation of the prevailing homosexual lifestyles of his own day. These uncertainties are not going
to disappear in a hurry – and, as I have hinted, it is very

peculiar that attitudes to them should have become a touchstone of orthodoxy, in a way that the New Testament gives little support to. The main thing is to have our eyes firmly on what is central and distinctive in both Paul and Jesus: sex is not everything, and there are imperatives more urgent where the Kingdom of God is concerned; but sex is capable of revealing God in the deliberate weakness of a love that entrusts itself to another with no prenegotiated limits of time and availability. That, says Scripture, is what sexual intimacy *can* be for humans. As so often with the New Testament, the question is thrown back to us: now what are you going to do about making such a possibility real?

Peter's Friends

AIDS, Shame and Suffering

□ □ □

Grace Jantzen

Job 7:11, 13–21

That is why I cannot keep quiet:
   in my anguish of spirit I shall speak.
   in my bitterness of soul I shall complain.

If I say, 'My bed will comfort me,
   my couch will lighten my complaints,'
you then frighten me with dreams
   and terrify me with visions,
so that strangling would seem welcome in comparison,
   yes, death preferable to what I suffer.
I am wasting away, my life is not unending;
   leave me then, for my days are but a breath.
What are human beings that you should take them so seriously,
   subjecting them to your scrutiny,
that morning after morning you should examine them
   and at every instant test them?
Will you never take your eyes off me
   long enough for me to swallow my spittle?

Suppose I have sinned, what have I done to you,
    you tireless watcher of humanity?
Why do you choose me as your target?
    Why should I be a burden to you?
Can you not tolerate my sin,
    not overlook my fault?
For soon I shall be lying in the dust,
    you will look for me and I shall be no more.

2 Corinthians 4:7–18

But we hold this treasure in pots of earthenware, so that the
immensity of the power is God's and not our own. We are
subjected to every kind of hardship, but never distressed; we
see no way out but we never despair; we are pursued but
never cut off; knocked down, but still have some life in us;
always we carry with us in our body the death of Jesus so
that the life of Jesus, too, may be visible in our body. Indeed,
while we are still alive, we are continually being handed over
to death, for the sake of Jesus, so that the life of Jesus, too,
may be visible in our mortal flesh. In us, then, death is at
work; in you, life.

But as we have the same spirit of faith as is described in
scripture – *I believed and therefore I spoke* – we, too, believe
and therefore we, too, speak, realising that he who raised
up the Lord Jesus will raise us up with Jesus in our turn, and
bring us to himself – and you as well. You see, everything is
for your benefit, so that as grace spreads, so, to the glory
of God, thanksgiving may also overflow among more and
more people.

That is why we do not waver: indeed, though this outer
human nature of ours may be falling into decay, at the same
time our inner human nature is renewed day by day. The
temporary, light burden of our hardships is earning us for

ever an utterly incomparable, eternal weight of glory, since what we aim for is not visible but invisible. Visible things are transitory, but invisible things eternal.

Psalm 102:1–11

When I was deciding to join the Society of Friends (Quakers) some years ago, one of the big influences – although I don't think he ever knew it – was John James, the clerk of the meeting. John was an unassuming man – a bit diffident – but Sunday by Sunday he and his partner Dugan would be at meeting for worship; and Sunday by Sunday he would greet Friends with obviously sincere pleasure. And almost every time I saw him, he would ask how I was doing and come out with some exclamation of praise. 'I'm proud of you,' he'd say – even if it was about only a small thing. Or, 'Grace Jantzen, I think you're marvellous.' His comments could be a bit over the top for what the situation warranted, but he always found a way to make me feel significant – more than just accepted. Even when I felt a bit foolish, John's pride in me was a steady source of pleasure that is still with me even though three years ago John died of an AIDS-related illness.

Did you see *Peter's Friends?* Ten years after their graduation, Peter invites his College friends to a New Year's Party. They aren't easy: one is alcoholic, another bulimic, one couple rows, another has recently lost a baby and both parents are neurotic about their remaining child. They all quarrel and fight. Towards the end Peter tells them he's HIV positive. What a great party! Peter was rather less fortunate in his friends than I was with John.

34

They seemed to think that friendship gave them the right to belittle one another, find each other's sore spots, and pick and poke at them until they were raw and bleeding. They hurt themselves and each other and fought and stormed and were the sort of house guests I for one would have been glad to have seen the back of. I didn't much like Peter's friends. And when at last he told them he was HIV positive, what did you think of their response? Well, to be sure, at least they didn't say, 'Gosh, are you gay? How *awful*!' – and I guess that's something. Some of them offered a rather lame, 'If there's anything at all we can do, just let us know' – and that's something more.

There wasn't condemnation and there wasn't isolation: to their credit, they were at their best rather than at their worst in the face of his announcement. But on the other hand, they clearly had no idea what to do with it. It was Peter – not they – who had to find the emotional resources to help everyone deal with it. Peter who had to propose the toast, Peter who had to comfort and reassure and eventually produce the picture of the past and give them something else to talk about. They didn't have it in them to build him up. They couldn't give him dignity and pride in himself, probably because it was in such short supply among themselves. It was as well that he had a good deal of dignity and pride already.

In my view, pride is something most of us could well do with a great deal more of – pride in ourselves, pride in each other, pride in our work and our achievements but also just in our being. Yes of course I know that Christianity has long taught the sinfulness and the perils of pride: wasn't it pride that caused the 'fall', pride that tops the list of the seven deadly sins? I think, though, that it is important to distinguish between pride and arrogance – of which there is a very great deal too much: the sort of arrogance that won't look at its own weak underside, that rides roughshod over other people's sensitivities, that is so busy attending to itself that it has no emotional space to build up someone else. But why are people arrogant? Why were some of Peter's friends arrogant? It was not because they had pride in themselves: on the contrary, I think it was precisely because they did *not* have pride, because they did not like themselves very well, and tried to cover themselves with the strips they tore off each other.

To be sure, some of them felt lots of guilt (and one or two swung violently from guilt to arrogance and back, partly depending on how drunk they were. . . . But just as arrogance isn't the same as pride, so I suggest guilt is not the same as shame. And just as we are often arrogant because we don't have enough pride, so I think we often carry around great loads of guilt without confronting shame. There's lots of talk about guilt (some of it rather cheap), but not much real consideration of shame. What is it to be ashamed? In my experience, a most wretched state. When I am ashamed of myself, it is because I have not lived up to my own standards of integrity or respect for others, ashamed because I would have expected better of myself, and I cannot be proud of what I have done. That's different from feeling guilty. I can feel guilty and resent it, because I don't think I should be made to feel that way; but if I feel ashamed of something, though I might well be miserable, I'd hardly be resentful. Again, it's all too tempting to try to cover up feelings of guilt by being arrogant: but I can't cover up feelings of shame by being proud of myself.

So shame is different from guilt. In fact, I want to suggest that while we can and do often feel *guilty* out of a low self-esteem and sense of being worthless, we can only really feel *ashamed* if we have some pride in the first place. Only if we have standards and a sense of pride in ourselves and one another can we feel that those standards have been betrayed, that we have not lived up to our best expectations: and *then* we are ashamed. In that sense, shame is a very mature response, mature because it rests on a developed sense of dignity and integrity, whereas guilt can be immature, squirming around in inadequacy. Quakers often speak of discerning 'that of God' in everyone, that sacred best which we do well to foster and take pride in, in ourselves and each other. And only as we discern 'that of God' do we also learn to discern that which is not of God, that which falls short. Pride and shame go together as mature responses; arrogance and guilt are prone to be equally immature. Peter's friends were pretty shameless and without much pride; instead they had plenty of guilt and heaps of arrogance and inadequacy.

But that, so far, is highly individualistic, as though we could just overcome guilt and generate pride by choosing to; and we all know that things are not that simple. None of us lives in a vacuum; it is within our social and linguistic structures that we are formed as speaking subjects and as subjects of desire, and consequently within those structures that our responses of guilt or arrogance, shame or pride are formed. Now, one of the ways in which a society can define itself is by contrasting itself to what it is not: not savage but civilised, not passive but competitive, and so on. By abjecting its other, seeing the 'other' as vilified and polluting, a society constitutes itself as pure, above reproach. Whether these 'others' really *are* foul or evil is not the point. A society can perceive itself as unstained by defining and defending itself against its alterities, who are thus made to bear its shame. They are seen as the ones who threaten it from without or pollute it from within; and they give rise to anxiety, dread, and quite irrational phobias.

Late capitalist society has for historical and material reasons constituted itself as though the norm of humanity were male, white, heterosexual and able-bodied. Those not conforming to this norm in various ways are seen as the 'other', and subordinated or abjected. Recent discussions of immigration laws in Parliament and the media have shown again the xenophobic compulsion to defend this island against the 'pollution' of people of colour. And those of us who are lesbian or gay know to our cost the extent to which we are perceived as contaminants, and the lengths to which society will go to try to keep itself 'pure': Clause 28, no gays in the military, no ordination of 'practising' lesbians or gay men to Christian ministry, and even calls for allowing discrimination against lesbians and gay men in housing and some forms of employment, as is already the case in some North American states. Too often the Churches have colluded, actively and passively, with such strategies of a threatened society, projecting shame onto those classified as 'other' rather than robustly challenging racism, sexism, and homophobia at their source. And when AIDS developed, it was seized upon by large segments of society (including, to their shame, some church leaders) as an occasion for further projection of shame onto those who were already suffering.

But as Michel Foucault insisted, every place of domination is also a place of resistance, a place where a reverse discourse can begin. Against the racism of the West, Black Pride has taken a stand; against homophobia, Gay and Lesbian Pride has refused the place of shame. If you have ever participated in a Gay Pride demonstration, or a march of Black and White together against racism, you'll know how empowering they are. Now, why 'Pride'? Why this word? Surely if what I am saying is correct, then 'pride' is exactly the right term around which the reverse discourse can be constructed: a term affirming worth and dignity and maturity. It is right for all of us, women and men, white and black, lesbian, gay and straight to be proud of who we are, to recognise, value and nourish that of God in ourselves and in one another. Black Pride, Gay and Lesbian Pride, enables us to resist together what is much more difficult to resist alone: the projection on to us of the idea that we are polluted and the polluters of society, that we should be ashamed of who we are rather than name and claim our selves and each other in maturity. This is more true, rather than less, in a world where AIDS has made its appearance, and where it is seen as an illness emanating from those perceived as such polluters: Africans, drug users, and gay men.

And as I have already said, it is only as we develop such maturity, such proper pride, that we will be able to recognise the standards we affirm and the integrity to which we aspire. This is not to say that we never have cause to be ashamed. But when we are, that shame will not be shame of our very being, as though who we are is polluting, but of the places where we fall short of 'that of God' in us, behaving toward ourselves and others in ways we can't be proud of, failing to delight in ourselves and one another, including our bodies and our sexualities, in the ways that proper pride calls forth.

Peter was a bit too good to be true – there's no reason to think that people who are HIV positive are plaster saints. But he had won through to a dignity and maturity which helped him discern what sorts of things one should rightly be ashamed of – using people, damaging people, lying – and what sorts of things to deal with without shame, even though they were not easy: HIV, the loss of his father, the possibility of his own early death.

When the film was over, my partner and I speculated about how the story might have continued, what it would have been like when Peter's friends left to go back home. And I found myself remembering some words of George Fox, which I thought might have been a seventeenth-century way for Peter to wave farewell: 'And this is the word of the Lord God to you all, and a charge to you all in the presence of the living God: be patterns, be examples in all countries, places, islands, nations, wherever you come . . .; then you will come to walk cheerfully over the world, answering that of God in everyone' (George Fox, *Journal*, 1694).

Prayer

Spirit of God,
You see our most public face and the secret thoughts
of every heart.
We bring the arrogance that is in us – and the guilt;
We bring the faith that is in us – and the doubt;
We bring the joy that is in us – and the sorrow;
We bring the pride that is in us – and the shame;

Peter's Friends

We bring the knowledge that is in us – and the
ignorance;
We bring the hope that is in us – and the despair;
We bring the courage that is in us – and the fear.

Spirit of God,
Give us grace to walk maturely in the way of Christ,
And strengthen us against all evil.
Amen.

(Adapted from *The Iona Community Worship Book*, Wild Goose
Publications/The Iona Community, Glasgow, 1991. Reproduced by
permission.)

When Harry Met Sally

Orgasm, Morality and Mysticism

❏ ❏ ❏

Angela Tilby

Song of Songs 2

– I am the rose of Sharon,
the lily of the valleys.

– As a lily among the thistles,
so is my beloved among girls.

– As an apple tree among the trees of the wood,
so is my love among young men.
In his delightful shade I sit,
and his fruit is sweet to my taste.
He has taken me to his cellar,
and his banner over me is love.
Feed me with raisin cakes,
restore me with apples,
for I am sick with love.

His left arm is under my head,
his right embraces me.

When Harry Met Sally

– I charge you,
daughters of Jerusalem,
by all gazelles and wild does,
do not rouse, do not wake my beloved
before she pleases.

BELOVED: I hear my love.
See how he comes
leaping on the mountains,
bounding over the hills.
My love is like a gazelle,
like a young stag.

See where he stands
behind our wall.
He looks in at the window,
he peers through the opening.

My love lifts up his voice,
he says to me,
'Come then, my beloved,
my lovely one, come.
For see, winter is past,
the rains are over and gone.

'Flowers are appearing on the earth.
The season of glad songs has come,
the cooing of the turtledove is heard in our land.
The fig tree is forming its first figs
and the blossoming vines give out their fragrance.
Come then, my beloved,
my lovely one, come.

Intimate Affairs

'My dove, hiding in the clefts of the rock,
in the coverts of the cliff,
show me your face,
let me hear your voice:
for your voice is sweet
and your face is lovely.
Catch the foxes for us,
the little foxes
that make havoc of the vineyards,
for our vineyards are in fruit.

My love is mine and I am his.
He pastures his flock among the lilies.

Before the day-breeze rises,
before the shadows flee, return!
Be, my love, like a gazelle, like a young stag,
on the mountains of Bether.

1 John 4:7–12

My dear friends,
let us love one another,
since love is from God
and everyone who loves is a child of God and knows God.
Whoever fails to love does not know God,
because God is love.
This is the revelation of God's love for us,
that God sent his only Son into the world
that we might have life through him.
Love consists in this:
it is not we who loved God,
but God loved us and sent his Son

to expiate our sins.
My dear friends,
if God loved us so much,
we too should love one another.
No one has ever seen God,
but as long as we love each other
God remains in us.

Psalm 100

Our readings from a collection of ancient oriental erotica
could provide final proof – for those wanting it – of the
moral degeneracy of the Church of England. It seems
unlikely that the Song of Songs – the Song of Solomon
as it is more often called – was actually written by
Solomon in spite of his many wives. No one knows who
wrote it in fact, or when, or why . . . or indeed how it
finds its way into the Hebrew Bible. This is the one book
which never mentions God, where the concern is fleshly
rather than spiritual. It was incorporated into the Jewish
Bible after the Fall of Jerusalem. There was some debate
about whether this was a book which would 'defile the
hands' – in other words whether it was really so charged
with divine inspiration that ritual washing was required
by those who read it. The great Rabbi Akiba helped get
it into the Hebrew canon declaring that 'all the ages are
not worth the day on which the Song of Songs was
written. All the writings are holy, but the Song of the
Songs is the Holy of Holies.'

So there it is. Erotic verses. Love songs of the orient.
From the beginning both Jewish and Christian
interpreters decided that it was not to be taken at face

value. If the Lord had disposed that the Song should be in the canon, it must be there as an allegory. Its real purpose was not to celebrate human, bodily love, but the love of God for Israel, for the Church, for the unique human soul. And this has remained true to this day. You won't find the Song in even the alternative readings in *The Alternative Service Book* at celebrations of the Holy Communion associated with the sacrament of marriage.

'Come then, my beloved, my lovely one, come . . .' Instead it conjures up the image of trembling virgins, brides of Christ, exchanging a wedding dress for a shaved head and a black habit. Or dour, married Puritans who would have been appalled at any hint of homo-eroticism praying to Christ as the Presbyterian Samuel Rutherford did: 'O that I had but Christ's off-fallings . . . that he would let the meanest of his love rays and love beams fall from him . . . a kiss of Christ blown over his shoulder . . . a shower like the thin May mist of his love, would make me green and sappy . . .'

The mystical traditions in Judaism as well as Christianity read this text as a celebration of the intimacy with which God pursues and woos his human prey.

And where does that leave human love, sexual desire, the attractions and passions which pursue and wound us all our life long? Both Judaism and Christianity have an investment in faithfulness and loyalty. Both, in that sense, are romantic religions, though Judaism has the edge on pragmatic common sense, Christianity on high-flown idealism. The film that provides an alternative text for this essay, *When Harry Met Sally*, is a wonderfully comic exploration of the struggle of romantic love in a fractured, fragmented world. The chorus of pathetic, glorious couples who interrupt the saga of hero and heroine reinforce a simple message: true love will always find a way. 'The winter is past, the rain is over and gone . . .'

So what does God make of Harry and Sally and their comic, romantic, erotic drama? And of the desires and passions of our own lives? Should we recover the Song of Songs as a celebration of human love or will it always remain an allegory for God and the soul? One of the early scenes in the film *When Harry Met Sally* illustrates the difficulty beautifully. Sally is complaining to Harry about her ex-boyfriend. He had noticed that she had designer knickers which blazoned forth the days of the week from Monday to Saturday. 'Where's Sunday?' he demanded, his suspicions aroused. Her response, that they didn't make Sunday knickers, failed to allay his worries. But why were there no Sunday knickers? Her answer, 'God', says it all.

God. God, that suggests, does not like human beings having sex much. It may be tolerated on other days, but on Sundays, God's day, it is forbidden. Somewhere in the post-Puritan consciousness of 70s' America lurked the belief that God is in competition with sex and desire for our attention and commitment. God, in other words, is a jealous God.

The roots of our fear of God's jealousy of sex go back to the faith of ancient Israel's covenant. It was an exclusive covenant. The God of Israel, unlike other oriental deities, had no heavenly consort. He was married to Israel alone. Those who gave in to temptation and worshipped the fertility deities of Canaan, were rudely condemned as adulterers.

Once this exclusive theology is in place a huge amount begins to be built on the sturdy foundations of human sexual repression. Monotheism produces monogamy. 'For better, for worse, for richer, for poorer, in sickness and in health . . . cleave thee only unto him/her, until death do us part'. These are the terms and conditions of the service of God, austere and beautiful and difficult for fickle human nature to comprehend, let alone fulfil.

And then there is that refinement of this austere tradition in celibacy, the permanent renunciation of sexual engagement. Was Jesus celibate? Or just unmarried? There's a question. Celibacy is often presented as the ultimate in human commitment to God. 'Come then, my beloved, my lovely one, come . . .' The marriage of the soul to the infinite, the mystic union of human bride and heavenly bridegroom.

What does this tradition say to us? Is God, indeed, jealous of our human loves? Is that why they are restricted, to mirror his narrow and all-embracing fidelity? Is there a competition going on between the love of God and the love of a human partner? Is that why the name of God cannot appear in the Song of Songs, and it cannot be part of the Bible unless it is all seen as a story of God? Does God want to be everything, or is God simply God? Is that why there is an embarrassing gap, a caesura if you like, a lesion between Christian spiritual experience and sexuality. I have been dreading pronouncing the 'O' word, which was part of my brief. I can say it outside a church building, not dressed in my Sunday best or in church I can speak of God, but the two languages still do not mix very easily. This is why Christianity is such a romantic religion: its finest flowers are built on the repression of sex.

Take champagne for example: who but a monk, Dom Perignon, could have invented it? The repression of air-filled wine under wire and cork, the outrageous knobbed bottle, the explosion of pleasure, the white foam, the outburst of human joy. What do you think is going on here?

I know it's customary to moan about sexual repression, to castigate Christianity for the damage that too strict a code of sexual behaviour has wrought in many human souls. Would that the Church had encouraged us to be more ordinary, and less heroic, more humble and less self-sacrificing, more gentle in recognising our need for animal comfort and bodily companionship.

Yet I want to say something else too. I remember the late 1960s and 70s as an era of sexual permissiveness. Everyone believed that the contraceptive pill had freed us from the repressions of our parents and grandparents. As a Cambridge undergraduate you almost felt obliged to demonstrate your freedom at every possible opportunity. When I look now at the films that were made then, and perhaps particularly at the television advertisements, for chocolate bars and hairspray, for new cars and even tea-cakes, I see how deeply they appealed to a particular kind of aggressive desire – which was hugely patronising to women, to children, to the old and unattractive, to the shy or the odd. It was sexual paradise, but a fool's paradise, and I don't entirely regret the puritanical feminism that put an end to the era of bushy sideburns and floral shirts.

Now, it seems to me, we have different problems with sexuality which revolve around commitment. We have lost our romanticism, our courage towards one another and towards God. To commit, to say, this is for life, is something we seem unable to do. We hear the call, 'Arise my love . . .' but we want a weekend break rather than a lifetime, with separate beds because we actually sleep better alone. I am thinking at the moment about people I know, Cambridge graduates and poor kids who left school without GCSEs. Those who have had it said to them, 'I love you, but I'm not in love with you. I care about you, but I don't want commitment' and have taken the honesty of their confession as a mandate for control either of sex, or time or affection or friendship – and because the other is needy, vulnerable, caring, endlessly hopeful – the relationship has ploughed on for weeks, months, years . . . until the one who was so honest in the first place finds a way out.

This is a desolation to which the Bible's ambiguity about sex seems to me to speak. We must live with the tension of duality: the Song of Songs as an allegory, and as a secular song. It is erotic and sexy, it is sacred and profound. Both are true, though not at the same time. God wants to be God for us, not to rival or supplant our human loves. It is sheer bad taste, said Bonhoeffer, to yearn for the infinite when you are in the arms of your spouse.

So, on the one hand is the glorious romance of the gospel of God. God, as the beginning and end of our desire, the Alpha and the Omega, to whom all hearts are open. And on the other a search for a human life-companion, a partner, a friend, a lover.

I believe that it is because God is for us, that we are free to take the appalling risks of human commitment, because God ratifies his promise that we can trust ourselves to love and be loved, even if things go wrong and fall apart. God does not expect perfection of us, but a certain fidelity and humility in which human passion and prayer are the doors to the Holy of Holies, the secret of the Word made flesh in which our human nature finds its greatest judgement and its truest hope.

And so, without fear that prevents commitment and the cynicism which spoils it: 'My dear friends, let us love each other, since love is from God and everyone who loves is a child of God and knows God.'

Blow Up

Pornography and Power

□ □ □

Margie Tolstoy

2 Samuel 11:1–5

At the turn of the year, at the time when kings go campaigning, David sent Joab and with him his guards and all Israel. They massacred the Ammonites and laid siege to Rabbah-of-the-Ammonites. David, however, remained in Jerusalem.

It happened towards evening when David had got up from resting and was strolling on the palace roof, that from the roof he saw a woman bathing: the woman was very beautiful. David made enquiries about this woman and was told, 'Why, that is Bathsheba daughter of Eliam and wife of Uriah the Hittite.' David then sent messengers to fetch her. She came to him, and he lay with her, just after she had purified herself from her period. She then went home again. The woman conceived and sent word to David, 'I am pregnant.'

1 Corinthians 6:12–20

'For me everything is permissible'; maybe, but not everything does good. True, for me everything is permissible, but I am determined not to be dominated by anything. Foods are for the stomach, and the stomach is for foods: and God will destroy them both. But the body is not for sexual immorality: it is for the Lord, and the Lord is for the body. God raised up the Lord and he will raise us up too by his power. Do you not realise that your bodies are members of Christ's body: do you think one can take parts of Christ's body and join them to the body of a prostitute? Out of the question! Or do you not realise that anyone who attaches himself to a prostitute is one body with her, since *the two*, as it is said, *become one flesh*. But anyone who attaches himself to the Lord is one spirit with him.

Keep away from sexual immorality. All other sins that someone may commit are done outside the body: but the sexually immoral person sins against his own body. Do you not realise that your body is the temple of the Holy Spirit, who is in you and whom you received from God? You are not your own property, then; you have been bought at a price. So use your body for the glory of God.

Psalm 32

A few years ago, every time you bought a book in the religious bookshop in Cambridge opposite King's College, the transaction was not complete until the title was read out into a tape recorder. It was entertaining; while browsing you were informed of what was bought . . . a brief glimpse into a private life. It was amusing until the day I purchased the book that is relevant to the topic of this sermon. I duly paid for it and the person read out the title, in what suddenly became an unnecessarily loud voice: *Dirt, Greed and Sex*. Heads turned and I may well have blushed. Was it pornographic literature? Not very likely. Not in a religious bookshop! But the title does provide an appropriate description of pornography and that is no coincidence. The full title explains that the subject is 'Sexual ethics in the New Testament and their implications for today'. It is written by L. William Countryman, Professor of New Testament Studies. The title, *Dirt, Greed and Sex*, gives a straightforward reference to important categories that play a crucial role not only in sexual ethics, but in the establishment of moral values in general. *Dirt* refers to the purity ethic, and is concerned with what is clean or unclean, or more accurately, this category establishes boundaries of decency. Overstepping these boundaries marks what is unclean, dishonourable, obscene. There is no universal agreement about what constitutes dirt. It is context specific. *Greed* is the cardinal sin of the property ethic; wanting more than your fair share, wanting to disown, taking what is not yours, trespassing on your neighbour's property. The categories of purity and property play a powerful role in sexual ethics and it is so obviously relevant when the subject of discussion is pornography. By pornography I mean the explicit visual or descriptive representation of sexual activity to stimulate erotic feelings. For some, pornography is a clear transgression of basic human conduct, for others it is harmless fun or just another way to make a living in an imperfect world. There may no longer be agreement in our society about the purity and property laws that apply to the expression of our sexuality, but Christians are committed to a moral order that provides clear boundaries. And pornography is out of bounds. Treating others as objects of pleasure is exploitation, even if consent has been given.

The purity laws and property laws of ancient Israel that applied to sex were very clear. Everything had its proper place. We come across both obedience to and the violation of the property and purity law in the reading of 2 Samuel 11: the story of King David and Bathsheba, wife of Uriah, the Hittite. Bathsheba had finished menstruating and bathing marked the end of her state of ritual impurity. Cleansing at that particular time was in strict obedience to the purity law. The description of King David observing all this from the roof of the palace, desiring and taking 'the woman who was very beautiful', is clearly erotic. There is no evidence of consent or resistance. What the King wants, he shall have. But then Bathsheba is given a voice in the story that disrupts: 'I am pregnant!' This is not what the King had in mind. She is no longer just an object of desire, but a human being. The consequences of this oversight are set in motion. King David tried to persuade Bathsheba's husband, a general in the army, to go home and lie with his wife so that the child to be born would appear to be his. But obedience to the purity law made him reject the offer. Uriah (like King David) was engaged in a war and sexual intercourse with your wife during that time made you unclean and therefore unfit for battle. Uriah was ordered to undertake a dangerous mission instead and was killed. That is no coincidence. Unrestrained sexuality is more often than not associated with violence, which can be either mental or physical. It adds to the excitement and to the devaluation of people which it requires. Robert Alter, in his book *The Art of Biblical Narrative* (New York, Basic Books, 1989), draws attention to this scene and remarks:

55

As a rule, when a narrative event in the Bible seems important, the writer will render it mainly through dialogue so the transitions from narration to dialogue provide in themselves some measure of what is deemed essential, what is conceived to be ancillary or secondary to the main action. Thus David committing adultery with Bathsheba is reported very rapidly through narration, with brief elements of dialogue, while his elaborate scheme first to shift the paternity to Uriah, and when that fails, to murder Uriah, is rendered at much greater length largely through dialogue. One may infer that the writer means to direct our attention to the murder rather than to the sexual transgression as the essential crime.

Well, up to a point. The one is entirely connected to the other. Basic laws concerning dirt, greed and sex were violated. Perhaps a woman reads this differently and notices that the writer directs our attention to the consequences of sexual transgression. The essential crime is the objectification of a human being. It diminishes both the transgressor and the transgressed, as the story illustrates.

Moving away from the Hebrew Bible to the Christian Scriptures, the first Letter of Paul to the Corinthians, is also concerned with dirt, greed and sex. In 1 Corinthians 6:12 Paul seems to suggest that in the new order, inaugurated by Jesus Christ, everything has been overturned: ' "For me everything is permissible"; maybe but not everything does good . . .'. What are we to make of this . . .? In 1 Corinthians 10:23–4 the same principle is repeated with an important addition: 'All things are lawful, but not all things build up. Let no one seek his

own good, but the good of his neighbour . . .' (RSV).
Paul's point of reference in 1 Corinthians 6 is very
specific. He is talking about the use of prostitutes by
male Christians and he brings the overthrowing of the
purity laws regarding food into the discussion of sex.
Paul points out that repudiation of the purity code does
not leave sex, like food, outside the range of ethical concern. He promotes the new understanding that believes
that it is only purity of heart and spirit that generates
right action. Consider, for example, what Paul writes
in the Letter to the Thessalonians:

> For this is the will of God, your sanctification; that you
> abstain from unchastity; that each of you know how
> to take a wife for himself in holiness and honour, not
> in the passion of lust like heathen who do not know
> God; that no man transgress and wrong his brother in
> this matter, because the Lord is an avenger in all these
> things, as we solemnly forewarned you. For God has
> not called us for uncleanness, but in holiness.
>
> (4:3–7 RSV)

The New English Bible's translation of this passage
renders the last line, 'So then, the person who treats
another as of no account is despising not a human being
but the God who has put his Holy Spirit into you'. It is
consistent with what Paul said in 1 Corinthians 6: 'Do
you not realise that your body is the temple of the Holy
Spirit, who is in you and whom you received from God?
You are not your own property, then; you have been
bought at a price. So use your body for the glory of God'
(vv. 19–20). This puts his opening remark that 'everything is permissible' into context. The liberating message
of the gospel, which is a restatement of the liberating

codes of conduct of the Hebrew Bible, points to the paradox, that total freedom leads to enslavement by the forces of disorder. Unless regulated, the transgression of purity and property codes (described in terms of laws of the heart) pervert sexuality, because it prevents sexuality from being a source of God-given delight and therefore an integral part of what it means to love and be loved.

When Paul says, ' "For me everything is permissible"; maybe, but not everything does good', he is talking about freedom from self-destruction. Christians associate pornography with the destruction of the self that is made in the image of God. This is not another disguised way to put people off sex and passionate expressions of love, it is a plea to treat our sexuality with care, even with reverence. It is a plea to be discerning in this delicate form of relationship.

Gloria Steinem's description of pornography is also useful, in a book of collected essays by women on pornography entitled *Take Back the Night* (edited by Laura Lederer, London, Fontana, 1983).

She helpfully contrasts it with erotica as she writes:

> Erotica is rooted in 'eros' or passionate love, and thus in the idea of positive choice, of yearning for a particular person. Pornography begins with a root 'porno', meaning 'prostitution or female captives', thus letting us know that the subject is not mutual love, or love at all, but domination and violence against women (though of course homosexual pornography may imitate this violence by putting a man in the 'feminine role of victim'). It ends with a root 'graphos', meaning writing about or description of, which puts still more

distance between subject and object and replaces a spontaneous yearning for closeness with objectification and voyeurism.

Gloria Steinem suggests that the difference is even more pronounced in film, when we see the actual encounter. She writes that when people are really making love 'there is usually a sensuality and touch and warmth, an acceptance of bodies and nerve endings ... of shared pleasure'. It becomes pornographic when there is oppression of one by the other. It may be through the use of inappropriate objects, of force or by way of humiliation that creates a relationship of conqueror and victim. Sex is used to reinforce an inequality or to create one. It carelessly and callously suggests that pain and humiliation are justified in the provision of particular erotic pleasure. It is sadistic. Erotica is about enhanced sexuality, pornography about power and sex as weapon. Behaviour that purposely injures another person, either physically or psychologically, is immoral. For many people today, adultery is immoral, because it breaks a promise of sexual and emotional fidelity. It is still about dirt and greed, about matter out of place, even though the dirt and greed are mainly connected with moral concepts. These ancient categories are still in force.

We know too little about the encounter between Bathsheba and David to make a clear judgement. Could she have rejected his advances? More than likely not, and the pattern of domination by the man of the woman is in place again and it is deeply degrading for the woman. Pornography endorses and promotes that state of affairs. Not all pornography is violent, but it perpetuates a damaging and cruel lie, namely that women's sexual life is in the service of men, that a woman's pleasure consists in pleasing men. Pornography lies explicitly about women's sexuality and through such lies misrepresents their humanity, their dignity and sense of self. It also lies about men in the same way. It perpetuates the association of aggressive sexuality with essential expressions of manhood. Both women and men suffer from the effects of this misleading presentation.

But the pornography industry is a very lucrative business with a vested interest in keeping it that way. They do not want people to know that loving, sensuous sex is so much better than the cheap-thrill variety.

And what of Antonioni's film, *Blow up*?

I cannot really say that I enjoyed the film, but it has some redeeming features. It provides a fascinating and depressing picture of the sixties, the time of Vietnam and young people innocently advocating making love not war. *Blow Up* contained some sex and a lot of sexual posturing, but no one makes love. The relationship between women and men portrayed is uneasy as well as exploitive. The sense of an approaching apocalypse is illustrated in the empty life of a self-possessed young man.

The film opens with two contrasting images: young and colourful people involved in the theatre of anti-war protest provides one, and the other is of a large group of men leaving a doss house, a scene oppressive and grey. Impoverished people on their way to work that is underpaid and undervalued. Suddenly another contrast is presented as one of the men steps out of line into an elegant car and into another life. He turns out to be an overpaid and overvalued fashion photographer, confident of his almighty power. He treats the women who work for him as 'his' models with contempt. Their bodies become images of submission and possession in his hands. He calculatingly fakes sexual arousal in order to extract more authentic images of coy sexuality: the captured woman as vampire and victim. It is a chilling exposé of male power and male sexual fantasy. It is pornography without explicit sex.

During a walk in the park, the main character watches a couple embracing and quarrelling. The camera gives him the excuse to be the voyeur and he takes many pictures. When he walks back to his car to go home, the woman runs after him and demands the film. He refuses. There is a sense of foreboding in the encounter. Upon returning home he immediately develops the photographs and notices something suspicious in the background of one of them. He enlarges the photograph and out of the blurred vision appears a man pointing a gun. The woman embracing the man is seen to be looking precisely in the direction of the pointed gun. The photographer becomes obsessed with his picture. He believes he may have interrupted a potential killer. But when he 'blows up' part of another photograph, he discovers what looks like a corpse. He rushes to the park to see the dead body and take more pictures. When he has located the corpse he feels intimidated and shocked. Is it possible that in that moment something that was blurred inside him is now 'blown up' and in that enlarged vision he now sees in his life a similar cold and lifeless reality? He turns away, alone, God-forsaken, bewildered. That's where the film ends. The audience has witnessed a life lived without moral boundaries, without notions of dirt and greed. It leads to the death of one's humanity, and that is at one and the same time the death of God within.

Psalm 32 was one of Augustine's favourites, and the Christian Church adopted it as one of the seven penitential Psalms. His emphasis is on sin and forgiveness. To sin means to be separated from that which gives life and that is an impossible burden to bear. Forgiveness allows a return to the source of life, a return to blessedness. Our sexuality is part of that blessedness. Sex is to be received with delight and thankfulness but it is a gift that requires great care. We are surrounded by careless, casual sex. Suggestive images of sensuous bodies are used to boost the sales of everything, from cars to ice cream. There is plenty of cheap gratification on offer and on public display. It creates a world of confused sexuality. Sex has become a consumer product, seductively packaged and presented. Pornography is merely an extreme example of this dehumanising process.

There is, of course, a lot of feminist literature on the subject. Catherine MacKinnon and Andrea Dworkin write eloquently on the subject with the objective of getting pornography outlawed (MacDworkinism). As an opponent of any kind of censorship, and equally concerned about pornography, Nadine Strossen, in her recent book entitled *Defending Pornography – Free Speech, Sex, and the Fight for Women's Rights* (London, Scribner, 1989), aims to combat MacDworkinite 'victim feminism'. Fascinating legal and moral arguments are put forward by both sides. The irony is, of course, that these interesting and lengthy discussions give the subject a respectability it does not deserve. And in that sense, the intensity of the debate is depressing. Sexuality has become a fashionable subject; a seemingly inexhaustible

topic for discussion and study. I do not think that this is
any longer liberating the inhibited. Pornography is at the
extreme end of a world which is obsessively preoccupied
with sexuality. Dirt, greed and sex no longer refer to
social conditions that strive to create a better world,
instead they have become flexible criteria concerned
with individual fulfilment. A book by Jeannette P. Gray,
called *Neither Escaping nor Exploiting Sex* (St Paul's, Mid-
dlegreen, Slough, 1995), is surprisingly refreshing and
even healing. The title is promising and the subject
'women's celibacy', intriguing. In the desire to choose
celibacy as an act of Christian witness, Jeanette Gray
draws attention to this neglected option. She writes: 'By
re-symbolising Christian discipleship as indwelling love,
a dynamic reshaping of celibate love is imagined. All
human love seeks union, promises mutuality but is less-
ened by the fear of its being taken. Celibacy is an
experiment in human love. It anticipates a love where
relating is not a risk, is always mutual and is integrated
as "indwelling" . . .' That is, of course, the love of God.

A Walk on the Wild Side

'Lesbigay' and Christianity

□ □ □

Elizabeth Stuart

Song of Songs 8:1–7

BELOVED: Ah, why are you not my brother,
nursed at my mother's breast!
Then if I met you out of doors, I could kiss you
without people thinking ill of me.
I should lead you, I should take you into my mother's
house, and you would teach me!
I should give you spiced wine to drink,
juice of my pomegranates.

His left arm is under my head
and his right embraces me.

LOVER: I charge you,
daughters of Jerusalem,
do not rouse, do not wake my beloved,
before she pleases!

Who is this coming up from the desert
leaning on her lover?

I awakened you under the apple tree,
where your mother conceived you,
where she who bore you conceived you.

BELOVED: Set me like a seal on your heart,
like a seal on your arm.
For love is strong as Death,
passion as relentless as Sheol.
The flash of it is a flash of fire,
a flame of Yahweh himself.
Love no flood can quench,
no torrents drown.
Were a man to offer all his family wealth
to buy love,
contempt is all that he would gain.

Romans 12:9–21
Let love be without any pretence. Avoid what is evil: stick to
what is good. In brotherly love let your feelings of deep
affection for one another come to expression and regard
others as more important than yourself. In the service of the
Lord, work not half-heartedly but with conscientiousness and
an eager spirit. Be joyful in hope, persevere in hardship; keep
praying regularly; share with any of God's holy people who
are in need; look for opportunities to be hospitable.

Bless your persecutors; never curse them, bless them.
Rejoice with others when they rejoice, and be sad with those
in sorrow. Give the same consideration to all others alike.
Pay no regard to social standing, but meet humble people

on their own terms. Do not congratulate yourself on your own wisdom. Never pay back evil with evil, but bear in mind the ideals that all regard with respect. As much as is possible, and to the utmost of your ability, be at peace with everyone. Never try to get revenge: leave that, my dear friends, to the Retribution. As scripture says: Vengeance is mine – I will pay them back, the Lord promises. And more: If your enemy is hungry, give him something to eat: if thirsty, something to drink. By this, you will be heaping red-hot coals on his head. Do not be mastered by evil, but master evil with good.

Psalm 13

St Elizabeth the Thaumatourgos or Miracle-Worker is little known in the West. A fifth-century Eastern saint renowned for her miracles, fasting and for managing to avoid a bath throughout the whole of her life, in many respects her life as told by hagiographers is unremarkable for a female saint except for one feature, the destruction of a serpent or dragon. For Elizabeth was a female equivalent of St George, indeed, her feast follows his on 24 April. When I first came across her story and read it in conjunction with his it struck me as an evocative model of lesbian, gay, bisexual, and transgendered spirituality. By that I mean the spirituality that has begun to emerge from those of us who have up to now been the object of ecclesiastical attention, analysis and debate. Tired of being talked about we have begun to find our own voice in conversation with each other and engage in theological reflection upon our own experience.

To tell the story of St Elizabeth in brief: when she was an abbess Elizabeth was given a convent by the Emperor

Leo I but it was inhabited by a dragon. The dragon had to be evicted in order that the community of religious women might have a home. St Elizabeth walked up to the door armed only with a crucifix. In what we can imagine as her best Barbara Woodhouse voice, she summoned the dragon out, it put its head out of the door, she spat at it and it immediately keeled over, dead. The relevance to lesbian, gay, and bisexual and transgendered spirituality lies in the contrast with St George, because I think that what these two saints represent is two different types of Christian authority. (For more theological reflection on the life of St Elizabeth and other female saints see Elizabeth Stuart, *Spitting at Dragons: Towards a Feminist Theology of Sainthood* (London: Mowbray, 1996).)

In his devastating analysis of the use of power in the Churches James Mackey (1994) has drawn attention to the way in which the Roman Catholic Church in particular (but other Churches are implicated by comparison) in matters of sexual morality behaves like an oppressive political regime, for the hierarchy suppresses the moral agency of the people. This is particularly clear in its treatment of homosexuality. The homosexual 'inclination' is pronounced to be 'an objective disorder' and a tendency 'toward an intrinsic moral evil' (Congregation for the Doctrine of Faith, *Letter to the Bishops of the Catholic Church on the Pastoral Care of Homosexual Persons* (Rome: 1986)). Celibacy is the only authentic path for the homosexual Christian. Those of us who are lesbian or gay are told who we are and how we are to behave and, as Mackey notes, if rules of behaviour 'are simply revealed to me, if they are put in such a way that I am prevented from judging them, much less arriving at them, then I am once more in the presence of force and not of authority.'

Churches, though perhaps more subtle and more anxious to be perceived to be more 'liberal' in their approach, actually use the same model. When lesbian and gay people are told that, even though their relationships may not be sinful, they fall short of the ideal of heterosexual marriage, and lesbian and gay clergy are told that, because they are called upon to uphold Christian ideals they must live celibate lives, these are clear denials of moral agency. Although almost every Church hierarchy affirms the primacy of individual conscience usually some way will be found of punishing those who use it, either through some sort of public discipline or the refusal to employ or through public or private 'nagging'. St George represents this type of power. He rides into a community thrown into disorder by a plague-bearing dragon but he only arrives when royalty is directly threatened by it. As a tribune he wears armour and bears a sword. He is protected by a system and comes to restore order to another system. The community is completely dependent upon him to save them. In one version of the story he lassoes the dragon and leads it into the city where he uses it to bribe the terrified townspeople into embracing Christianity. Having done so he rides off into the sunset. The story of George is the enforcement of power on a vulnerable group of people. This model of authority grates against the teaching on leadership found in the Gospels where power is collapsed into servanthood.

The story of St Elizabeth represents a different kind of authority. It is not, to use the terminology of Starhawk and Pamela Cooper-White, 'power-over' but 'power-with' (see *The Cry of Tamar: Violence Against Women and the Church's Response* (1995), p. 32). Elizabeth was not an agent of super-powers seeking to 'save' communities with which she had no connection. She had no interests in bolstering authority structures or holding communities to ransom, she needed a safe space for herself and her sisters. She was at the heart of the situation. She asked for bread and was given a stone. She needed a home for herself and her community but it was tainted by what was inside of it. She therefore acted for herself and her community. But Elizabeth had no weapons or armoury or delegated authority, indeed as a woman she came from a position of positive non-authority. Yet she defeated the dragon with her own self – her voice, her spit and feet – armed only with a crucifix which she held before her as she walked into her home. Power-with arises from a recognition of what Matthew Fox has called 'original blessing', a recognition of God's image and goodness within you. It is the self-confidence that comes from the realisation of one's dignity as a child of God. Few of us have it because we are still defined primarily as sinner (rather than as good person distorted by sin) in Christian discourse. When it does come upon us, usually mediated through the love of others, it inspires a new way of relating to others grounded in mutuality, negotiation and consensus rather than force or control. (For a more detailed discussion of power and sexuality see Elizabeth Stuart and Adrian Thatcher, *People of Passion: What the Churches Teach About Sex* (Mowbray, 1997), ch. 5.) But, it could be argued, Elizabeth did not negotiate or try and reach a consensus with the dragon. The dragon is not a person, it is a force, a power that prevents the sisters enjoying basic justice, safety, community and a home.

Like St Elizabeth those of us who are 'queer' (to use the term adopted by many gay and lesbian people to refer to the non-heterosexual) and Christian believe we are offered a home in a Church which is occupied by a beast that will destroy us and whose presence infects the house – and that beast is homophobia. Faced with this prospect we have two options, one is to go off and build ourselves another home which is a noble and entirely justifiable thing to do, even though that is exactly what the dragon and his servants want us to do. Or we can enter the house and attempt to live with the dragon either by choosing to live in rooms which he does not often visit, or pressing ourselves into the shadows so as to become invisible to his gaze. It is easier for some to hide in the shadows than others – gay men seem to blend into the rich splendour of the Church's wallpaper better than lesbians. Bisexuals and transgendered people stand out like luminous socks. The problem with this approach is that, as in the story of St George, the dragon requires ritual sacrifice to keep his house in order and no one is safe. And particularly tragic is the sight of people who are so gripped by the dragon's rule that they voluntarily sacrifice themselves by suppressing, denying or seeking to change their sexuality. But a growing number of us are refusing to compromise with homophobia any longer and also refusing to be evicted from our rightful home. This is because like Elizabeth as communities we have found 'power-with', we have found our voice, spit and feet. We have reclaimed our dignity and authority as children of God. Indeed, we even have a creation myth to pinpoint the moment when that happened – the Stonewall riots in New York in June 1969; at that moment we like to say we became subjects, we began to trust and reflect upon our own experience. And so like Elizabeth we stand on the boundary, unarmed, unsupported and extremely vulnerable to attack because we are so visible. Unlike George but like Elizabeth we have no armour to protect us, no external authority to support our stand. Scripture, tradition and the full authority of the Church do not protect us. Unlike George we have no horse, no power to carry us above what confronts us. Like the authors of Psalm 3 we are deeply vulnerable to attack and despair for people say to us as they said to the Psalmists, 'There is no help for you in God', and often it is easy to believe that. It is also easy to despair because so often the emperor refuses to believe the dragon exists. These days all Churches condemn homophobia but very, very few will acknowledge its presence within their own walls. It is something like St George's dragon that roams around 'out there'. Just as I can remember people of my parents' generation saying with real sincerity, I am not a racist but I wouldn't want my child to marry one/live next door to one/ to have one as my doctor because they smell/take all our jobs . . . So it is very common in Church circles to hear people say, 'I am not homophobic but . . .' These people have no concept of what homophobia is because they have not been at the receiving end of it nor are they much interested in listening to those that have because for them the declaration of non-homophobia provides a cloak with which to screen themselves from the reality of queer lives. It prevents them having to recognise the connections between the fire-bombing of a lesbian household or the knifing of gay teenagers on the street and the ecclesiastical pronouncement that homosexual people are disordered or fall short of the ideal. It protects them from the call to stand in costly solidarity with the victims of homophobia.

Yet Elizabeth did summon up enough courage and authority to defeat her dragon. Her courage came from her commitment to her sisters. Similarly 'queer' people find their courage to stand on the boundaries from solidarity. From the kind of passionate friendship that develops between people who are vulnerable, who only have each other. This kind of authority is clearly evident in the film *Walk on the Wild Side* where two women have to learn to trust the experience of their own love for one another in the context of violent male heterosexuality. It is miraculous that they do so.

Elizabeth's authority comes from herself and it is expressed in the bodily form of her own voice, spit and feet. Yet, it is also more than just her authority. She carries a crucifix before her to acknowledge that God is the source and content of her power. In the Gospels Jesus too conveys God's authority through his person in his voice which often summons out demons, his spit which heals and his feet which walk on water – all of which generate opposition and allegations of allegiance with the forces of darkness. When 'queer' people claim a voice in Church and society we are accused of trying to recruit the innocent into our evil ways or of trying to claim special privileges and rights. When we march we are accused of flaunting ourselves or being unnecessarily confrontational. When is spitting a violent act and when is it a healing act? What others perceive to be violent confrontation, gay and lesbian people perceive to be spitting at dragons, exorcising homophobia. Exorcisms were never tea and cake affairs, they were confrontational and messy.

Elizabeth's power comes through her body. The experience of marginalisation, of being deprived of any external authority, has prompted many lesbian, gay and bisexual Christians to draw upon their common experience, their body knowledge and to detect the traces of divine authority within it. Like the lovers of the wonderfully erotic Song of Songs we have encountered God in the very place where others see only distortion and decay – in our passion. The standard English translation of verse 6 of chapter 8 of the Song interestingly eliminates the only reference to God in the entire poem. The 'flames of passion' described in verse 6 are in Hebrew the 'flames of Yahweh', of God. It is in the midst of their love which may be heterosexual but, as Heather Walton has so nicely put it, 'is not straight in a straightforward way', but is deeply subversive: it is inter-racial, perhaps even incestuous, certainly disapproved of by family and society. (See 'Theology of Desire', *Theology and Sexuality* no. 1 (September 1994).) But nevertheless God dwells in and indeed is the passion that binds them together. The authority of the lovers, of Elizabeth and the lesbian, gay and bisexual comes from deep body knowledge of God, of encountering God in our subversive passion and it is with this knowledge that we encounter the dragon.

Of course Elizabeth could have done a St George: captured the dragon and set it on or at least threatened the emperor who had caused her so much trouble. It is the easiest thing in the world to imitate those who hurt you. I think that lesbian and gay people are beginning to learn that Paul's instructions in Romans 12:14–21 are right. There is no point responding in kind to those who oppose you – homophobia is a phobia, it is irrational even though it might disguise itself in rational discourse, which is why so much debate about homosexuality in Christian circles is about as useful as a discussion between a tarantula and an arachnophobe. All we can do, like Elizabeth, is summon the dragon and present him with our body theology. Having been for so long at the end of uncompromising authority should also engender within us a theology of humility. We may be wrong. At times we certainly will be wrong. We have yet to see if, like Elizabeth's scaly adversary, the dragon will shrivel up. But like many queer Christians my instinct leads me to trust that it will and to act accordingly. As Christians we worship a God who became, in Dietrich Bonhoeffer's famous phrase, not an idea or a law or a proposition but a body. Maybe this is the way that God works generally by revealing herself in our bodily experience, as 'power-with' rather than 'power-over' – Christianity's pathological distrust of the body has obscured this possibility. No one is claiming that 'queer' Christians have a greater monopoly on truth than anyone else but if God does work through bodies then the voices, the spit and the feet of these people need to be privileged in Church discussion about our lives. We are claiming our power, our dignity, our privilege as people made in the image of God. Ironically, it is our marginalisation and oppression that have driven us to this realisation, which is why we can understand something of the irony of the last beatitudes in Matthew 5:10–12: blessing has come through calumny and persecution. We are claiming our home and we are not the only ones: the whole spectrum of women, black people, Asian people, disabled people, people doing theology in solidarity with animals and the earth are doing the same, reflecting upon God from the heart of their bodily experience – dragons everywhere should prepare for a rough ride.

Carnal Knowledge

Men and Sexuality

◻ ◻ ◻

Anthony Dyson

(with Martyn Percy)

2 Samuel 13:7–17

David then sent word to Tamar at the palace. 'Go to your brother Amnon's house and prepare some food for him.' Tamar went to the house of her brother Amnon who was lying there in bed. She took dough and kneaded it, and she made some cakes while he watched, and baked the cakes. She then took the pan and dished them up in front of him, but he refused to eat. Amnon said, 'Let everyone leave me!' So everyone withdrew. Amnon then said to Tamar, 'Bring the food to the inner room so that I can eat what you give me.' So Tamar took the cakes which she had made and brought them to her brother Amnon in the inner room. And as she was offering the food to him he caught hold of her and said, 'Come to bed with me, sister!' She replied, 'No, brother! Do not force me! This is no way to behave in Israel. Do not do anything so disgraceful! Wherever should I go? I should be marked with this shame while you would become disgraced in Israel. Why not go and speak to the king? He will not

76

refuse to give me to you.' But he would not listen to her: he overpowered her and raped her.

Amnon was then seized with extreme hatred for her: the hatred he now felt for her was greater than his earlier love. 'Get up and go!' he said. She said, 'No brother! To send me away would be worse than the other wrong you have done me!' But he would not listen to her. He called his personal servant. 'Rid me of this woman!' he said. 'Throw her out and bolt the door behind her!'

1 Corinthians 7:32–40
I should like you to have your minds free from all worry. The unmarried man gives his mind to the Lord's affairs and to how he can please the Lord: but the man who is married gives his mind to the affairs of this world and to how he can please his wife and he is divided in mind. So, too, the unmarried woman and the virgin gives her mind to the Lord's affairs and to being holy in body and spirit: but the married woman gives her mind to the affairs of this world and to how she can please her husband. I am saying this only to help you, not to put a bridle on you, but so that everything is as it should be, and you are able to give your undivided attention to the Lord.

If someone with strong passions thinks that he is behaving badly towards his fiancée and that things should take their due course he should follow his desires. There is no sin in it: they should marry. But if he stands firm in his resolution without any compulsion but with full control of his own will and decides to let her remain as his fiancée then he is acting well. In other words, he who marries his fiancée is doing well and he who does not better still.

A wife is tied as long as her husband is alive. But if the husband dies she is free to marry anybody she likes, only it must be in the Lord. She would be happier if she stayed as she is, to my way of thinking — and I believe that I too have the Spirit of God.

Psalm 45:1–9

I want to begin with an autobiographical note. Some twenty years ago I was appointed a consultant for the Lambeth Conference and participated in its proceedings. During the conference there was a day off enabling a small number of bishops to make the journey from Canterbury to St George's Chapel, Windsor Castle. One of the bishops was from a diocese in South-east Asia, where there was a sharp political conflict, and the Church was under various forms of pressure. The bishop made his tour of the Chapel and exited. He was palpably distressed. Asked for his reactions to the Chapel, he did not refer to the architecture, the beautiful choral singing, or to the special side-chapels. His comment was addressed directly to the conflict the Chapel embodied: that between a spiritual house on the one hand, and on the other, as a house for swords, coats of arms, knights and other military trappings. The bishop gave a radical interpretation to the Chapel. Most of us present, quite liberal-minded, focused on the aesthetics and treated the other elements as 'toys' or decoration. But for the bishop, the symbolism was deeply disturbing.

Another person was present. She was a deacon of the American Episcopal Church, negotiating the difficult transition between imposed diaconal ministry to that of a priest, if indeed that were to be possible. She had been obliged to undergo interviews exploring her psychological balance and her sexuality. Earlier, she had attended the mid-morning Sung Eucharist, but when I had come upon her not long after, her face was red with tears. She was surrounded by a small group who were explaining the virtues and necessity of the liturgy in this setting. She, for her part, was only aware of the profound alienation she had experienced, based solely on gender-bias. For her, Holy Communion was being radically denied its meaning. Even the most liberal apologists at the time could only suggest a limited role for women. The woman deacon sobbed in dismay. The South-east Asian bishop declared the place fatally compromised. Everybody else said the place was beautiful; but it could not be so. What it included and excluded at the time amounted to a deep rejection of true communion, 'led' by men.

Men get a bad press these days. Perhaps they deserve it? Allegedly poor at fathering, unable to express their emotions, repressed, patriarchal, domineering and spoilt; it seems almost impossible to redeem the concept of maleness. The litany of complaints against masculinity are almost endless. There seems to be no way of winning, as a man. Those who embrace feminism and show signs of being in touch with their emotions, or are self-declared New Men are dubbed 'soft' by the political right. Those who stick to a form of gung-ho maleness, remain traditional-patriarchal, or are self-confessed New Lads, have to live with tags such as 'pathetic' from the left. As for gay men: don't even try.

Popular culture, it seems, knows no happy medium. Men are base and beast; women are human. The humorous BBC TV programme *Men Behaving Badly* is undoubtedly a parody of this. But, like all parodies, there is a correspondence with reality. Moreover, there is some sense of role models being offered. Gary and Tony play rather sad, pitiable figures in the show, and their own lack of male role models makes their inadequacies seem rather endearing. It's OK to be a bit of a lad, to revel in boyish immaturity. If you're a real girlie, you'll put up with it, because men have eventually to assume leadership and responsibility. So can we have some fun now, please?

This is not a new genre of caricature for masculinity. The post-modern and mocking irony of *Men Behaving Badly* is prefigured by the late modernist male sexual predator. In James Bond films, or in Jack Nicholson in *Carnal Knowledge*, we meet men who know what women want better than they know themselves. This is the world where refusal of sex is usually deciphered as coy foreplay, and ultimately to mean 'Yes'; the seduced woman becomes soppingly grateful for the man who could *really* discern her true desires. It is a male fantasy – but one few men would wish to entertain these days in more politically correct environs.

Masculinity is in a state of crisis. Furthermore, the Bible seems to be of little help. The models of maleness do not appear to be ones that should in any way be copied. True, the virtues of courage, sacrifice, grace and the like are there in abundance. (Yet these are not particular to men.) But when it comes to considering how men behave as men, towards women, the picture is cloudy at best. Amnon's selfish lust, possessiveness and violence are shameful. Like David, he seems to assume he can have whatever he wants: if seduction fails, try rape. St Paul, far from reconfiguring his maleness in Christ – at least in 1 Corinthians 7 – seems to assume that men know best, and that women are *naturally* bonded to men, with an implied subservience.

In the title of this essay, 'men' is not mankind, but 'man' in contrast to 'woman'. Sexuality is a concept with notoriously fuzzy borders: there is no agreement over its definition. Theologically, however, there is such a thing as 'personhood': it is a given, and is related to the *imago dei*. But this givenness is interpersonal, and so implies a personal and social embodiment that is mysterious. Sexuality is structured around personhood; it is not just something you have, but a fundamental way of being in all things. So, can masculinity be reconfigured in personhood?

There are many men who claim to have seen the light, and to be able to stand on the side of women. But it is never as simple as that. The first thing to say about New Men is that they are reactions to feminism, which claims to have discerned and disclosed patriarchy. The New Man generally imagines himself to be a rebel, a convert from 'hard-line' masculinity who has rejected violence and domination. Yet what emerges is not a rejection of masculinity, but an adaptation of it. New Men, all too frequently, remain in charge: power structures have not been transformed. The New Man is simply a sensitive version of what went before. In effect, post-modernity has produced a hybrid masculinity that is better suited to retain control. As one feminist writer puts it, 'the New Man ideal is manipulated to become a reactionary figure, co-opted into the service of patriarchy'.

There seems to be a stalemate. St Paul appears to offer a happy hunting ground in which chauvinist assumptions can allegedly be located. But this is to ignore a central Pauline theme, that in all that separates human beings (including gender, sexuality, etc.), Christ brings together body and personhood, creating a new kind of possibility for all. Naturally, we must ask how this is possible for men as men. What, if anything, can be said about maleness and spirituality, that does not collude in processes of alienation and domination? Several points arise.

First, gender-identities are basically irreducible. Although some men have attempted a deconstruction of their personal lives, have begun to penetrate some of the mysteries of maleness, and to reject the 'normal' way of being a man, there is only so far you can go. Our gender-identities are contradictory; they do not simply 'complement'. Symmetrical relations between the sexes exist, but competition for space and power remain. Whatever 'male liberation' is, it is not the same as liberation for women. There may be certain interiorised social structuring of maleness that men wish to shake off, but women's liberation is still about exterior oppression and access to equality. All too frequently, this is made into a deeply interior affair for women as well. In other words, personal male abrogation of power does not necessarily lead to greater social power for women. It just creates a vacuum that a different hybrid of male can fill.

Second, the idea of a 'fixed, masculine self' is a false ideology. Like all ideology, some will be liberated by its articulation, whilst others are oppressed. This will often be especially true of gay men. The masculine myth is an obviation of diversity, entrapping men and women in an encumbered code of 'what it means to be a man'. There is a struggle with a lie about continuity here. Thankfully, good work on the development of sexuality (sociological, anthropological, historical, psychological, etc.), along with more generous attitudes to gay men, have helped many see that their sexuality and person-hood is a more fluid affair, even if their gender was apparently 'fixed'.

Third, New Male movements that offer a redemption of maleness need to be handled with care. Robert Bly's best-selling *Iron John* (New York, Addison-Wesley, 1992) capitalised on a perceived misrepresentation of male-ness, that many men felt angry or hurt about. Bly invites men to 'attain the full dignity . . . of the deep masculine'. For Bly, this excludes being guided by women, or attempting to conform to social 'norms' of maleness, including the 'wet' and allegedly culturally-imposed New Man. The subtlety and appeal of Bly's work rests in its invocation of a male spirit. Men should reject the 'gentle Jesus, meek and mild', and embrace the angry, muscular Jesus of authority, who overturned tables and rebuked opponents.

Last, and linked to the above point, the spiritualised versions of men's movements do not seem to offer serious help either. Organisations such as *Promise Keepers*, an American, ecumenical movement that is proving to be increasingly influential, seem to define themselves in opposition to so-called 'liberal' trends. Thus, feminism is denounced for emasculating men. Even midwives are criticised for de-skilling men during the birth of their children. The whole movement, under the guise of redeeming the authentic, godly male, turns into an exercise of sexism and patriarchy. The gloss – and it is only a gloss – is the welcoming of emotions and their expression. But there is no doubt that the movement is simply an attempt to sell one version of being male, consecrate it, and then impose it again over women.

If any serious thinking about maleness is to be done, it is important to recognise that concepts of gender are never simply contingent, or decided on in a haphazard way. At any given moment, gender reflects the material interests of those who are in power. For example, Arthur Brittan (*Masculinity and Power*, Oxford, Blackwell, 1989) suggests that it might be helpful to distinguish between three types of maleness: masculinity, masculinism and patriarchy. Masculinity refers to the fluctuating male behaviour that may be culturally related. Masculinism is the ideology that 'naturalises' male domination. It assumes heterosexuality is normal, that there are fundamental differences between male and female, and accepts the division of labour by gender. Patriarchy is its praxis, resourced from religion, politics or other public ideologies. All share a belief in male 'essence', believing in the coherence of man, and ultimately his supremacy.

What emerges out of this discussion is a sense that 'masculine' and 'feminist' spirituality, whatever they might be, are not straightforwardly gender-specific. Feminist spirituality is nearly always, partly, about redeeming lost or hidden images of divinity, reclaiming power for women, and ensuring that their embodiment and experience of God is not marginalised. 'Masculine' spirituality, by contrast, is not engaged in the same war at all. It is either a defence of the *status quo*, or, an attempt to redefine (alleged) male supremacy. This is because a masculine aura of competence persists, with images of masculinity present in our most intimate and ordinary communication. Thus, there is 'men's work', 'men's recreations' and the alien 'male experience'. The recent writings of Nick Hornby (*Hi-Fidelity* (1995) and *Fever Pitch* (1992), published by Indigo) characterise this genre well. Yet expressions of masculinity are culture-specific, not ontological. In our society, every aspect of 'masculine' character is contradicted by another culture. Any kind of manual labour, craft or skilled job can be linked to one sex in one culture, but be different in another. Feminists have always taken the view that gender is cultural and social, and therefore historically accountable. Thus, there is no *universal* masculine identity: the epochs vary from time to time, place to place.

So, what can be said about men, sexuality and spirituality to conclude? In one way, not much. Feminist spirituality is still speaking to men, and our primary task must be to listen, listen, listen – and only then to respond. A right to reply and 're-balance' male supremacy seems premature, and most likely unjust. If there is a genuine male spirituality, it will be something that is ultimately inclusive of women. Perhaps it might begin with a deeper acknowledgement of our shared but particular personhood, that corresponds to the *imago dei*: the Trinity. Here, all three persons may be conceived of as 'male'; these are the dominant metaphors of tradition. But what the Trinity stands for at a deeper level is a theology of community, harmony, friendship, openness, order, mutuality and service. It is dynamic relationship, constantly self-aware *and* fully attentive to others. In short, 'I no longer call you slaves or servants, but friends' (John 15:15). Making more of deep friendship and of committed relationality is the only way forward for men and women alike. It signals the end of competition and the start of co-operation; the celebration of difference, but the promise of true rapport. For God is the author of peace, and the lover of concord.

All about Eve

Women and Sexuality

◻ ◻ ◻

Mary Grey

Genesis 3:13–16
Then Yahweh God said to the woman, 'Why did you do that?' The woman replied, 'The snake, tempted me and I ate.'

Then Yahweh God said to the snake. 'Because you have done this,

> Accursed be you
> of all animals wild and tame!
> On your belly you will go
> and on dust you will feed
> as long as you live.
> I shall put enmity
> between you and the woman,
> and between your offspring and hers;
> it will bruise your head
> and you will strike its heel.'

To the woman he said:

> I shall give you intense pain in childbearing,
> you will give birth to your children in pain.
> Your yearning will be for your husband,
> and he will dominate you.

All about Eve

Revelation 12:1–6

Now a great sign appeared in heaven: a woman, robed with the sun, standing on the moon, and on her head a crown of twelve stars. She was pregnant, and in labour, crying aloud in the pangs of childbirth. Then a second sign appeared in the sky: there was a huge red dragon with seven heads and ten horns, and each of the seven heads crowned with a coronet. Its tail swept a third of the stars from the sky and hurled them to the ground, and the dragon stopped in front of the woman as she was at the point of giving birth, so that he could eat the child as soon as it was born. The woman was delivered of a boy, the son who was to rule all the nations with an iron sceptre, and the child was taken straight up to God and to his throne, while the woman escaped into the desert, where God had prepared a place for her to be looked after for twelve hundred and sixty days.

Psalm: Hymn to Wisdom (Janet Morley, 1994)

We know all about Eve, don't we? We know her as temptress, seductress, as the icon of female sexuality, vilified, demonised, 'the Devil's Gateway' – according to Tertullian – the dark other to the respectable Adam. As those of you who have seen the film *All about Eve* also know, she is no friend of other women; rather, she jumps on the bandwagon of competing for the man, and the job, in this case an ageing woman and her lover. Thus she removes the ground from the feminist myth of sisterhood. (And you know that this is an age–old scenario inviting sarcasm against women.) The negative personifications of Eve throughout Christian tradition are numerous and although they run across the complex gamut of relationships between women and men, yet they have one common theme running through them: we know Eve as the *bad woman*, foil to Mary, the mother of Jesus, the *good woman* of the Christian tradition par excellence. As Virgin Mother she is held up as the true icon of female sexuality, despite all the biological difficulties involved! Fra Angelico's *Annunciation* says it all: centre-piece we have the angel bringing the invitation to the young girl at prayer, and the suggestion of the overpowering of the Spirit; to the left, as backcloth, is the angel with the fiery sword driving Eve out of Eden. The message is summed up in the great medieval hymn, *Ave Maris Stella*, 'Eva's name reversing' – the Ave of Annunciation cancels out the curse of Eve.

Does Eve fare any better in Jewish tradition? It is true, she does not play a centre-stage role, as in Christianity. In fact, Eve, the bad woman, does not appear until comparatively late (and is not mentioned by name). In the Wisdom of Sirach, it is said, 'Sin began with a woman, and thanks to her we must all die' (25:24). And in the Rabbinic tales, she appears not as seducer, more often as a weak and silly creature. There is a parable of Adam and Eve, where

> Adam is like a husband who filled a cask with figs and nuts. Before fastening the top, he put a scorpion in it. He said to his wife: 'My daughter, you have free access to everything in the house, except for this cask, which has a scorpion in it.' After he left an old neighbour came in to borrow some vinegar. She asked the wife: 'How does your husband treat you?' The wife answered: he treats me with much kindness, save that he does not permit me to approach this cask which

contains a scorpion. 'It contains all his finery,' the old
woman said, 'he wishes to marry another woman and
give it to her.' What did the wife do? She inserted her
hand into the cask and the scorpion bit her. When
her husband came home he heard her crying out with
pain. She told him that the scorpion bit her and he
said: 'Did I not tell you that you can have anything in
the house except this cask?' (Gensis, Rabbah 17)

So in this story cited by Nehama Ashkenazy (1986) – in
which you will have identified many mythic echoes –
we have the whole episode reduced to a domestic
squabble, and Eve's thirst for knowledge diminished to
idle feminine curiosity. The question is: could the Jewish
tradition only afford to de-demonise Eve, who, after all,
continues a highly-respected career as *Mother of the
Living* – and motherhood, we are told in Christianity,
is the way for female sexuality to be redeemed! – her
escapades with the serpent put behind her, *because behind
Eve lurks the ghost of Lilith, who is much more threatening*?
Lilith, rather than Eve, is the real icon of rejected female
sexuality. Lilith was the legendary first wife of Adam,
who was allegedly banished as being too independent,
with a mind of her own; and, as such, on the one hand,
she has delighted the imaginations of feminist theologians, both Jewish and Christian, and has taken the
demonic weight off Eve. But on the other hand, she
continues to be the rejected 'other' of female sexuality.
She appears as the Kabbalistic figure, who joins men at
night and bears them demonic offspring. In fact, interestingly, a sixteenth-century illustration of Josephus's *Jewish
Antiquities* depicts Lilith with the face of a woman and

the body of a snake lurking behind the trees in the garden and spying on Adam and Eve.

Nor is Lilith confined to Midrash and Kabbalistic lore but reappears in modern dress, for example, in Amoz Oz's story, *Strange Fire* (in *Where the Jackals Howl*, 1964). Here she is named Lily, *Esh Zarah*, the enigmatic, even demonic character in Jerusalem, which is presented as a physical and moral battleground of the forces of good and evil. As a modern incarnation of Lilith 'her entire being evokes the darkness of the night'. She is the link between the modern Jerusalem and the sphere of evil and chaos that takes over at night with which she has mysterious affinity. She is both seductress, moral corrupter – she seduces her future son-in-law – and psychological other. Furthermore, she is also the embodiment of 'the black and abysmal side of life and of the human psyche', and, as the title *Strange Fire* suggests, she is the catalyst that releases the 'subterranean forces of chaos and madness in her surroundings'.

Tragically, this archetypal figure – Lilith/Lily/Eve – has obligingly acted, in our Western tradition at least, as the demonic embodiment of the subliminal male primordial fear of female sexuality. Think of the terrible Queen of the Night, in Mozart's *Magic Flute*, of Morgan Le Fay of Arthurian legend, of the numerous vulnerable single old women vilifed and burnt to death by the Great European Witch-hunt, and of the way sexism joins with anti-Semitism in the depiction of the Jewish woman as the rejected other: for example, in Sir Walter Scott's *Ivanhoe*, the story demands that the Jewish Rebecca, daughter of Isaac the Jew, is the real heroine whom Ivanhoe loves. But our culture's choice is Rowena, the golden-haired Anglo-Saxon, just as Christian culture has chosen the asexual figure of Mary as antithesis to the fallen carnality of Eve/Lilith.

It is time to recognise that, as the title of Helena Kennedy's book puts it, *Eve was Framed* (1990). Whether as demonic Lilith, or Eve the temptress who has truck with serpents, or as the great and terrible Mother beloved of Jungian psychology, *women are framed* as more sexual and less rational; they are framed by Augustine as disordered symbol of human nature, and therefore in desperate need of control if there is to be any civilised society at all. And we see how that control works in the text of Paul's Letter to Timothy, where, deliberately recalling that Eve sinned first and not Adam, the writer, allows that 'women will be saved through bearing children' (1 Timothy 2:15 RSV). Precisely. The Church has tried very hard to channel female sexuality into safe waters – namely, marriage and procreation – and those who would not be channelled, but have called for distinctive meanings for female sexuality as part of the fullness of being a woman, are easily vilified. By continually framing Eve as fantasy object, as plaything, as insatiable for sex, as competing with a younger woman for a man (as in the film in question), fear as to the irrationality, power and uncontrollability of sex continues to be projected onto one sex and fuller and more satisfying meanings elude both men and women.

Is there no escape from rigid control and scapegoating? One way is to look again at the story we have just read (Genesis 3:16) and realise that this is not a story about sexuality as sin at all, but a story of creation's disordered relations with God. Nor does it set Adam (good) against Eve (bad). Adam is rather passive in the whole story: indeed many medieval pictures show him

sleeping through the event! The connection with Eve
and the serpent – frequently depicted with the head of
a woman – is rather to be seen against the Near Eastern
background where the serpent is a symbol of wisdom,
and Eve, a figure of wisdom associated with it. It is
interesting that Eve talks to the serpent and is eager for
knowledge. In the passage from the Book of Revelation
(included on p. 87) we see the figure of the woman with
the serpent or dragon at her feet – here the serpent
functioning as symbol of vanquished evil (with deliberate reference to Genesis 3). And part of this evil is that
human beings are set over against animals. Bestiality is
another way of speaking of demonised sexuality.

But it is not enough to reclaim the story of Eve, Mother
of the Living and possibly serpent goddess, Eve who
thirsts for wisdom. Not enough to remove the Eve/Mary
antithesis. For what this does not do is to remove the
power implications of distorted sexuality today. What
Elizabeth Schüssler Fiorenza names *kyriarchy*, the rule or
domination of the lord (which orders unjust patterns of
social relating, sexism, racism, economic oppressions),
means that the vilifying of female sexuality – outside the
safe area of legal marriage – is necessarily the official
line to justify control, to demand obedience, to condone
domestic violence and even rape because of so-called
'provocative' behaviour, and to undergird the whole
realm of prostitution. To give a personal example: in my
work in India, as part of a charity 'Wells for India' which
my husband and I set up, we are working with prostitutes in Rajasthan. They serve the truck drivers who
thunder along the highway from Delhi to Bombay. Yet,
mostly they have been kidnapped as young girls from
their poverty-stricken homes in different parts of India,

with promises of money and marriage. Other people – including the police force, which gains massive bribes – benefit from their earnings. And we came into the story because of their children. Little girls from five years upwards were about to be dragged into a life of prostitution. They are not the playthings of Hollywood directors – their story does not warrant a film. Somehow the myth of Eve the temptress or the demonic Lilith is shockingly out of place when you see that here, at the heart of it all is not sex, but power, money, greed. And the end of the road is that these women and their children will die – or be killed.

For while a few theologians and a few philosophers such as Luce Irigaray are frantically busy reclaiming or rewriting the texts – and this is a major work and a crucial one – women and girl children on a massive global scale are actually dying, because the collective kyriarchal story supports the expendability of women. You don't need me to give global statistics on the infanticide of girl babies or deaths from sex tourism.

As well as the theoretical work, there is a desperate need *to live out* new expressions of human sexuality in distinctive female meanings. And I suspect these are not so mysterious, or mystifying as the gurus would have us think. 'What do women want?' said Freud, and did not listen for an answer. Women want their bodies to be respected, in all the processes of becoming a woman and growing old ... We want an end to being objects of pleasure, fantasy, manipulation and exploitation. An end to being bought and sold to satisfy either male sexual need, or greed. We seek justice and mutuality in our human relationships. We long for an end to the cheapened and degraded versions of eros, sexual desire, currently fashionable. We yearn for safe spaces, spaces of trust, where sexuality can be expressed as tenderness, in compassion, in joy, in friendship. And we ground our hope for this in the eros of God, whose eros for us is consistent, passionate and grounds us in our sexual reality, our distinctive female sexuality:

'Open to me, my sister, my love,
my dove, my perfect one,
for my head is wet with dew,
my hair with the drops of the night.'
(Song of Songs 5:2b)

It is the eros of God, who, in a paraphrase of Catherine Keller's words (1986), as the *molten core of our heart's desire*, in the darkness of exploitation and the reality of shame, energises our courage and our quest.

Afterword

Sexuality, Spirituality and the Future

◻ ◻ ◻

Martyn Percy

In response to the question whether or not he believed sex was dirty, Woody Allen is alleged to have said: 'It is if you are doing it right.' Linking sex to dirt is a common enough trend within contemporary society, in spite of education and openness. Sex, or sexuality, is a contemporary 'category' that often describes behaviour that it is not polite to talk about. It is frequently seen as an 'area' to be steered clear of, and must certainly not be allowed to get too close to another category such as 'spirituality'. It should be clear by now that 'categories' as such, are at best generalisations, and at worst mistakes. Furthermore, it should also be obvious that 'spirituality' and 'sexuality', as forms of embodiment, cannot be separated without leading to some sort of schizophrenia. It was Foucault who pointed out that our classification of certain medical conditions is socially and historically related as much as it might be clinically defined (*Madness and Civilisation*, 1961): what is now 'mad' may once have been 'mystical'. Society can and does determine these categories to some extent, even in the privacy of our consciousness.

In a different way, Mary Douglas has shown that what counts as 'dirt' is a subject for the fluid market of social perception. Understanding what made things dirty or clean formed the basis for her work in *Purity and Danger* (1966), in which she argues that through concepts of pollution and taboo, society affirms its basic social relations. Thus, what is 'dirty' is not just dirt or mess, but 'matter out of place . . . dirt is never a unique, isolated event . . . where there is dirt, there is a [socially-defining] system' (p. 48). So, it is not earth that is dirty, but earth on the carpet: what is dirty depends on a system of classification. Thus, sexual activity in the bedroom is somehow 'normal', but in the kitchen or library becomes something else . . . exciting, odd or disgusting, according to taste. In terms of sex and sexuality, it is always having to shake off its profile based on dirt, which has no doubt arisen for many reasons.

Meanwhile, spirituality struggles with its apolitical reputation for cleanliness and niceness. Consequently, body and soul are kept apart. If the social, and to some extent the false boundaries between these two categories can be negotiated, the genuine possibility of a spiritual-sexual tapestry being embodied in society and in individuals starts to materialise. This might help society rid itself of some its taboos, and others of their hatred or shame. Still others may benefit by simply being able to be more open about themselves, instead of living a 'double life', where public and private are divorced. One member of the clergy I know was recently described as being 'so far in the closet, they are almost in Narnia'! Auden sets the agenda well when he writes:

May I, composed like them
Of Eros and of dust,
Beleaguered by the same
Negation and despair,
Show an affirming flame.

W.H. Auden, from 'September 1, 1939', in *Poems, Essays and Dramatic Writings, 1927–1939* (Faber & Faber), p. 283.

This book began life as a series of sermons. Obviously, this makes for some of the contributions being more polemical than systematic. Yet the purpose has always been to explore some key contemporary issues, rather than deal out dogma to dilemmas. Consequently, an afterword cannot be a conclusion; it can only set down some of the broad issues that might affect the ways in which we discuss sexuality and spirituality in the future. Typically, many prefer to keep these 'subjects' apart as we have noted. Yet it cannot remain so for much longer: the integrity of the Church requires a deep and ongoing dialogue that will start to converge towards understanding and respect for others.

Understandings of sexuality in contemporary society are in a state of flux. Modernist debates about nature or nurture have given way to the politics of choice. The post-modern world mistrusts the search for underlying truths, and contents itself with surface meanings. Sexually speaking, this is giving rise to a number of traits. A sexual relationship might not necessarily belong to a committed relationship: the pleasure principle seems to have overridden the need to love and be loved. The fragmenting and decentering of moral-religious narratives is also mirrored in sexual narratives. 'Meaning', 'significance' and 'truth' are becoming *personal* terms of endearment, which in turn has caused a peculiar casualness in sexuality *and* spirituality. Coupled with this is a willingness to experiment with experience and distrust personal identity 'sedimenting': 'monogamy' is a temporary arrangement, with sexual selfhood no longer held to be secure. Personal gratification is becoming the focus of social and sexual relations: the end of this is naked individualism. Yet society is already beginning to discover that individualism, though 'free', is a lonely dancer. What is needed is an ethic, a spirituality or even a public rhetoric whereby persons begin to think of themselves in terms of relationships: how they are formed by them, how they form them thereafter, and how others are formed through them. A Christian spirituality, especially an incarnational and Trinitarian one, may have much to offer to this situation.

The problem is that one can never 'just' have sex. It is an activity where culture meets with biology; body, self and society interact; where head and heart mix, contradict and agree. Sex is politics: how you express your desire and to whom betrays your needs, wants and hopes. Sex can also be guilt, aggression and frustration, besides sublime, creative and redeeming. Ironically, it is the 'place' where in losing control you find yourself, and where in gaining control you can lose the other. It is a spiralling tension and union: cacophony and harmony, pleasure and pain, joy and sorrow, laughter and tears, rebellion and conformity, indifference and passion – all bound together. It is a kind of faith: going beyond knowledge and into relationship, allowing yourself to have and to hold, to belong and to be cherished. Perspectives are hard to rationalise, and the sheer intensity of sexual experience and the complexity of sexuality may well dissuade some from critical reflection. Yet an appreciation of how we are both sexual and spiritual may help us to delight in the God in whose image we are made.

This could begin with a recognition that sexuality and spirituality share a language in the present. Perhaps we should even go further, and say that good theology has some resonance with good sex. Both involve mutuality, listening, attention to the other, exteriority, exchange and expression. Both are to do with desire, passion, engagement and energy. Both involve a degree of willingness – to be vulnerable and open; then again some harmony, yet uncertainty. Finally, agony and ecstasy are to be understood, and then worked with. It can be no accident that the language of worship (or worth-ship) and sexuality most obviously reaches its climax in marriage services, where union with God, union with another and delight in love are celebrated to the full. (Although, as we have noted earlier, it is also redolent in many mystical traditions.)

The key lies in seeing sexuality and spirituality as different but equally legitimate ways of *relating*: we are made for relationship, with God and with others. It is in our relationships with others that we find true fulfilment as human beings. Beyond this is a recognition that we are loved by God with what Mary Hunt (1991) calls a 'fierce tenderness' that encourages us to be mutual and responsible in our relating. Just as there is no hierarchy in the Trinity, but openness, mutuality and love between three persons who are one, so are our own relationships and personhood to be patterned. Just as Christ did not cling to equality, but emptied himself, so are we to serve others. Just as the Spirit inspires, liberates and transforms, so are we to be present to those around us. Just as God is order and love, passion and judgement, so are we to care for others. Our sexuality can manifest that divine love, and can be part of the paradigm of religious knowing.

Turning our sexuality towards God in this way may sound like a heavy task, yet it is true to the 'directional plurality' I hinted at earlier. Consequently, there must be a reminder that sexual fulfilment comes through deep, lasting and absorbing relationships. (However, it should be understood that certain kinds of social pressure, applied externally to sexual relations amongst minority groups, do not always allow or encourage long-term relationships. The resulting 'culture' of apparent infidelity can then be demonised even further by the majority.) Although we have not talked about sex and ageing, it is important to grasp that far too many moral or religious discourses on sex – popular and academic – assume that all adults essentially have regular, similar and 'normal' sexual appetites. This is plainly not so: the young, the old, some who are disabled and many others are excluded by this assumption. An emerging sexuality brings energy, poses questions, and takes risks. A maturing sexuality, like a maturing spirituality, may look less vigorous as time goes by, yet can constitute something far deeper in what it expresses and receives, and ultimately comes to know. Sexual relationships, whether good, bad or indifferent, to some extent help configure our identity as people. Even for those who are celibate, sexuality is never ultimately obviated. As both Rowan Williams and Angela Tilby suggest in their essays, it is just controlled, and channelled differently.

Turning sexuality Godwards can also raise questions of abuse and forgiveness. There is one sense in which any history of abuse inevitably involves an account of behaviour whereby the sexual activity is out of synchronisation with the relational commitment, and mutuality is destroyed. It is at this point that the associated promises of sexual behaviour are broken, inequality and deception set in and sexuality and spirituality are divorced, often at great cost to the parties involved. Notions of guilt and innocence quickly polarise people, and can lead to retribution, false reconciliation, or the endless silences of guilt and habit that spin unnoticed into future relationships. As the authors of a remarkable book on incest suggest (*Secrets in the Family*, Lily Pincus and Christopher Dare, London, Faber & Faber, 1978, esp. pp. 86ff. and 116ff.), there may be more holistic ways of dealing with abusive patterns and behaviour, besides punishment, which lie with a community that is profoundly understanding and forgiving.

Forgiveness, I would suggest, can never just be about forgetting the past. It is about remembering the past in ways that no longer constrain and dictate the future. It has a place for anger, and for addressing the past in those terms, but it is not ultimately beholden to this. Not even Jesus had the strength to forgive his abusers – all he could cope with was asking God to do this for him as he was tortured and betrayed, and then as the three of them faced their capital punishment (Luke 23:34ff.). Yet serious abuse does not always end in a 'death': there is the hope of resurrection, reconciliation and the promise of paradise. Thus, forgiveness, for the body of Christ, is a resurrection event: it is an ongoing act, a freeing of the yesterdays to make possible a new tomorrow. The logic of Jesus' own forgiveness is that he neither condemns nor condones the sexual sinner (cf.

John 8:1–11, Luke 7:36–50, etc.), but instead restores them to community by recognising the corporate nature of sin and the mutuality of guilt. This, in turn, invites the Christian community to ponder how it is to be a community of *love*, with all that implies about tolerance and grace. The church, as the social form of the Truth (or the body of Christ), is to be a redemptive revelation, not a punitive disclosure. Only when it is that sort of community can spirituality and sexuality be properly approached, as appropriate ways of relating to the other and to the self.

So, a true spirituality that is linked, synthesised even, with sexuality may be able to arrest the failure that so often distorts relationships, and blots out love. It may see that in the profound risks we all take in love and life, there will be failure, success, triumph and tragedy. 'Spirituality' is a term that usually describes the combination of beliefs and practices of an individual or group. At the heart of its study is the probing of the relationship between the 'inner' and 'outer' person. If the Church is to be the body of Christ, and is in turn made up of many different bodies, then it is clearly critical that sexuality and spirituality are in harmony. A divorce between the two colludes with the double-standards and moral fragmentation in society; it reinforces the notion that there can be no 'truth' or 'real' Christian voice that can speak for everyone. In terms of sexuality, the Church cannot speak to society if it cannot be honest with itself. And if it fails in this, there can be no prospect of society listening to what it has to say about spirituality. Consistency of belief and behaviour is much needed.

At this point, some might be tempted simply to re-impose a crude sexual ethic on all God's people, based on a certain way of reading a certain number of biblical texts. This guarantees a spirituality that is public, albeit in a 'shotgun' style. In short, it advocates certainty in the face of ambiguity and plurality. Plainly, this won't work: what becomes public might turn out *not* to be true. There is little that is certain about our sexualities, and it is uncomfortable to face this reality with others, which is why so many consign it to the realm of privacy. Our sexuality is usually something that goes on in the basement of our lives, hidden well away from the neighbours, and even ourselves. Yet the vocation to become more 'in the image of God' requires these rooms to be opened up to the light of Christ, and for the whole house to be 'a temple of the Holy Spirit'. The dualism between the 'inner' and 'outer' is to go, lest it harbour double-standards. Our sexuality and spirituality are to become like a seamless robe. This may sound fine in theory, but how is it to be done? There are a myriad of ways forward at this point, but I would like to suggest just three.

First, the church is to *be* a social ethic, not just 'have' one. This requires a moral consistency. Jesus was the *friend* of sinners; the thief is with him in paradise; the prostitute is given the honour of anointing him. Living as the welcoming, open and inclusive Christ is costly because it is a risk of faith. It alienates the prevailing power-interests, and works for those who are 'demonised' by society. When the church is established, one of its first tasks is to interrogate the standards and demands of the establishment. Yet typically the church short-changes itself and society at this point by failing to be dialogical: it adopts a moral 'policy' for those who 'fall short of God's grace' instead of living as though it is the body of grace. This is not friendship as Jesus understood it: it is 'treatment', and at a distance from reality. Correspondingly, it approaches some sins as though they were in a special category of their own, placing, for example, divorce and sexual sin on a pedestal, whilst being largely silent about other less visible sins that leave millions bonded in debt, poverty and despair. (A Roman Catholic colleague of mine underlines this by pointing out that he can absolve a murderer, but requires a special faculty from the bishop to forgive a woman who has had an abortion.)

Second, being a sexual ethic requires a radical kind of incarnation. It must recognise that sexual desire and expression are God-given, and then try and channel it in appropriate ways. Part of the witness of the church is to recognise that God is already at work in society, ahead of the mission of the church. If there are more tolerant attitudes to homosexuality or to gender-sensitive issues at work in society, God may be speaking to the church *through* society. The church must recognise that laws or literal readings of texts may not be as persuasive as compassion, honesty and openness. An over-concern with the imposition of tradition instead of befriending society as it is, may turn out to be the sure path to irrelevance. When was the last time the church affirmed the world in its relationships, and celebrated the honesty, integrity and fidelity that are beyond its own particular customs? The desire to control seems to supersede the willingness to learn.

Third, there has to be more recognition about the complexity of our sexuality and spirituality. If a selection of texts and traditions are not to be imposed in a simplistic manner, they none the less remain as part of the material that constitutes Christian faith. At the same time the 'core values' of Christianity (assuming there ever could be real and *total* agreement on these) need constant re-assessment in the light of the accelerating changes in society. The genius of Christianity has always partly lain in its focused directional plurality centred on the person of Jesus Christ, as well as in its mutatious adaptability: the knack of *re*-forming to speak to each new generation afresh, in culturally relative terms. The third millennium will seriously challenge that ability with the accelerating shifts in culture. With society captivated by an increasingly consumerist-led, information technology-driven and post-modern culture, religion is in danger of becoming a largely private affair. In turn, this will keep sexuality in the basement, making genuine public discourse difficult or meaningless.

If Christianity wishes to keep its hold of its claim on public and universal truth, it will need to begin thinking here. How can it live as the body of Christ for all people? How can it guide people in their sexual and spiritual quests? The whole story of creation, incarnation and redemption teaches us that God desires us as we are, indeed, as though we were him. If we can grow into that whole-hearted love of God, knowing that 'we love because he first loved us', we, as the body of Christ, may be that body of grace God wants for the world. It is in that same body that sexuality and spirituality can co-exist, converge and grow together. It is not so much a hope as a prayer:

> I rejoice in my sufferings for your sake, and in my flesh I complete what is lacking in Christ's afflictions for the sake of his body, that is, the church . . . make the word of God fully known, the mystery hidden for

ages and generations but now made manifest to his saints. To them God chose to make known how great among the peoples are the riches of the glory of this mystery, which is Christ in you, the hope of glory. (Colossians 1:24–8, RSV)

Appendices

A. The Bible and Homosexuality

◻ ◻ ◻

Some Notes from the Ontario Centre for Religious Tolerance

HTTP://WWW.KOSONE.COM/PEOPLE/OCRT/
HOMBIBL.HTM

In biblical times, same-gender sexual interactions could take many forms. Among them:

1. Kings of conquered tribes were sometimes raped by the invading army as the ultimate symbol of defeat and humiliation.
2. Some non-Jewish tribes in the area had male prostitutes in their temples that may have engaged in same-sex activities; this horrified the ancient Israelites.
3. It is reasonable to assume that many loving gay and lesbian relationships existed, but these would normally have been conducted in secret.

Only the third type would have any similarity to today's gay and lesbian consensual, committed, loving relationships.

Many versions of the Bible exist in the English language. Each reflects the world view, beliefs and mind sets of its translators. Their personal biases condition their work. There is an additional complexity facing translators: today's society is very different from that of biblical times. It is

107

sometimes difficult to find a current English word that matches a Hebrew or Greek term.

Many words have been translated from the original Hebrew and Greek texts as 'homosexual', 'sodomite', 'homosexuality'. However, most (perhaps all) of the references bear no similarity to today's lesbian and gay partnerships. By carefully reading the original texts and considering the societies in which they were written, one comes to surprising conclusions:

• The Bible has a lot to say about temple prostitution.
• It talks about being kind to strangers in a way that has been incorrectly interpreted as referring to homosexual acts.
• It says almost nothing about homosexual feelings.
• It says nothing about sexual orientation. The writers of the Bible assumed that everyone was heterosexual (or 'straight'); the concept of sexual orientation was not developed until the late nineteenth century.

The Bible does make occasional references to activities which have been translated as homosexuality:

• Genesis 19 describes how two angels visited Sodom and were welcomed into Lot's house. The men of the city gathered around the house and demanded that Lot send the visitors to the mob so that they might 'know' the angels. The Hebrew verb *yada* (to know) is ambiguous. It appears 943 times in the Hebrew Scriptures (Old Testament). In only about a dozen of these cases does it refer to sexual activity; it is not clear whether the mob wanted to rape the angels or to meet with them, and perhaps attack them physically. From the context, it is obvious that their mood was not friendly. Lot refused, but offered his two virgin daughters to be heterosexually raped if that would appease the mob. The offer was declined. God decided to destroy the city because of the wickedness of its inhabitants. The angels urged Lot and his family to flee and not to look back. Unfortunately, Lot's wife looked the wrong way, so God killed her because of her curiosity.

- God was apparently not critical of Lot for offering his two daughters to be raped. However, God was angry at the other inhabitants of the town. He destroyed Sodom with fire and brimstone (sulphur). He presumably killed all of the men in the mob, their wives and other adults, as well as children, infants, newborns, etc. It is unclear from these few verses whether God demolished the city because the citizens:

1. were uncharitable and abusive to strangers
2. wanted to rape people
3. engaged in homosexual acts, or
4. whether the punishment was for this single act involving Lot, or because of long lasting sinful behaviour

The Church has traditionally accepted the third explanation, and believed that the sexual activity was habitual. In fact, the term 'sodomy' which means 'anal intercourse' was derived from the name of the city, Sodom. But the first explanation is clearly the correct one. As recorded in Matthew 10:14–15 and Luke 10:7–16, Jesus implied that the sin of the people of Sodom was to be inhospitable to strangers. In Ezekiel 16:48–50, God states clearly that he destroyed Sodom because of their pride, their excess of food while the poor and needy suffered, and their worship of many idols; sexual activity is not even mentioned. Jude disagreed; he wrote that Sodom's sins were sexual in nature (v. 7). Various biblical translations describe the sin as fornication, going after strange flesh, sexual immorality, perverted sensuality, homosexuality, lust of every kind, immoral acts and unnatural lust.

We are faced with the conclusion that the condemned activities in Sodom had nothing to do with sodomy.

☐ Leviticus 18:22 states: 'Thou shalt not lie with mankind as with womankind: it is abomination' (KJV). The term 'abomination' (*to'ebah*) is a religious term, usually reserved for use against idolatry; it does not mean a moral evil. The verse seems to refer to temple prostitution, which was a common practice in the rest of the Middle East at that time. *Qadesh* referred to male religious prostitutes. (See the discussion of Deuteronomy below.)

☐ Leviticus 20:13 states: 'If a man also lie with mankind as he lieth with a woman, both of them have committed an abomination; they should surely be put to death . . .' (KJV). The passage is surrounded by prohibitions against incest, bestiality, adultery and intercourse during a woman's period. But this verse is the only one in the series which uses the religious term 'abomination', it seems also to be directed against temple prostitution.

These passages are part of the Jewish **Holiness Code** which also:

• permits polygamy
• prohibits sexual intercourse when a woman has her period
• bans tattoos
• prohibits eating rare meat
• bans wearing clothes that are made from a blend of textiles
• prohibits cross-breeding livestock
• bans sowing a field with mixed seed
• prohibits eating pigs, rabbits, or some forms of seafood
• requires Saturday to be reserved as the Sabbath

Churches have abandoned the Holiness Code; it is no longer binding on modern-day Christians. They can wear tattoos, eat shrimp, and wear polyester-cotton blends largely without violating this particular section of the Bible. Although this code is obsolete for Christians, many clergy

still focus on those passages which deal with homosexuality.

☐ Deuteronomy 23:17 states, 'There shall be no whore of
the daughters of Israel, nor a sodomite of the sons
of Israel' (KJV). This is an 'error' by the authors of the
King James Version. The word *qadesh* in the original text
was mistranslated as 'sodomite'. *Qadesh* means 'holy
one' and is here used to refer to a man who engages in
ritual prostitution in the temple. There is little evidence
that the prostitutes engaged in sexual activities with
men. Other Bible translations use accurate terms such as
'shrine prostitute', 'temple prostitute', 'prostitute' and
'cult prostitute'.

☐ Judges 19 describes an event much like that at Sodom.
This time, an unnamed Levite visited the town of Gibeah
with his slaves and concubine. He met an old farmer
and was made welcome. A gang of men appeared and
demanded that the old man send out the Levite that
they might homosexually rape or assault him. (It is again
not clear what the precise meaning of the verb 'to know'
was.) The old man argued that they should not abuse
the visitor. He offered to give them both the Levite's
concubine and his own virgin daughter to be heterosexually raped. The mob accepted the former, raped her all
night and finally killed her. The Levite sliced up her
body into twelve pieces and sent one to each of the tribes
of Israel. This triggered a war between the inhabitants of
Gibeah and the Israelites during which tens of thousands
died. There was no condemnation against the Levite for
sacrificing his concubine, or for committing an indignity
to a body. Judges 20:5 emphasises that the aim of the
mob was to kill the stranger – the ultimate act of inhospi-
tality. It appears that these passages condemn abusive
treatment of visitors. If they actually refer to homosexual
activity, then they condemn homosexual rape; they have

nothing at all to say about consensual homosexual relationships.

☐ I Kings 14:24 and 15:12 again refer to temple prostitution. The original word *qadesh* is mistranslated as 'sodomite' (homosexual) in the King James Version, but rendered as 'male prostitute', 'male cult prostitutes' and 'male shrine prostitutes' in more accurate versions. As mentioned before, there is little evidence that homosexuality was involved. Again, the text has nothing to say about consensual homosexual relationships.

☐ In Romans 1:26 and 27, Paul criticises sexual activity which is against a person's nature or disposition. This passage has been interpreted in many ways:

• Most biblical scholars believe that these verses condemn all gay and lesbian activity, whether casual or in committed relationships.

• Some people believe that St Paul is criticising orgiastic homosexual activities, but has nothing to say about homosexual activity within long-term partnerships.

• Some believe that St Paul is referring to homosexual temple prostitution, done in the worship of the goddess Aphrodite, and that a careful study of Romans 1 reveals this connection.

• A minority of scholars interpret the passage differently: in Greek society of the time, homosexuality and bisexuality were regarded as a natural activity for some people. Thus Paul might have been criticising heterosexuals who were engaged in homosexual activities against their nature. He might not be referring to homosexuals or bisexuals at all.

Traditionally, people have carried their beliefs about sexual orientation to this verse and interpreted the passage accordingly. The verse appears to be somewhat vague, and perhaps should not be interpreted as a blanket prohibition of **all** same-sex activities.

☐ In I Corinthians 6:9 Paul lists many activities that will prevent people from inheriting the Kingdom of God. One has been variously translated as effeminate, homosexuals, or sexual perverts. The original Greek text reads *malakoi arsenokoitai*. The first word means 'soft', the meaning of the second word has been lost. It was once used to refer to a male temple prostitute (as in the verses from the Hebrew Scriptures/Old Testament described above). The early Church interpreted the phrase as referring to people of soft morals, i.e. unethical. From the time of Martin Luther, it was interpreted as referring to masturbation. More recently, it has been translated as referring to homosexuals.

☐ 1 Timothy 1:9 again refers to *malakoi arsenokoitai* which has been variously translated as 'homosexuals', 'sexual perverts', etc. Again, the original meaning of the text has been lost.

☐ Jude 7 refers to the people of Sodom as 'giving themselves over to fornication and going after strange flesh'. 'Strange flesh' has been variously translated as 'perverted sensuality', 'unnatural lust', 'lust of men for other men', and 'perversion'. Again, it is unclear what is being referred to here. Some biblical scholars interpret this as referring to an ancient Jewish legend that the women of Sodom engaged in sexual intercourse with angels.

In summary:

☐ Homosexual activity in the temple by male prostitutes is clearly prohibited by the Hebrew Scriptures (Old Testament).

☐ Homosexual activity in general **may** have been prohibited at the time by the Holiness Code, but that code no longer binds Christians today.

☐ St Paul considered at least some male and female homosexual acts to be forbidden, but it is unclear precisely which acts are included. He may have been referring to temple prostitution, or to people who are not innately gay, lesbian or bisexual engaging in homosexual acts. One should note that Paul also condemned women preaching (1 Corinthians 14:34) or wearing gold or pearls (1 Timothy 2:11). He also accepted and did not condemn the institution of slavery. Some Christians feel that his writings are not a useful guide for ethics and morals in the twentieth century.

☐ Jesus made many hundreds of statements regarding belief and behaviour. However he never mentioned homosexuality.

☐ There are two biblical same-sex relationships (one between two women, the other two men) reported in the Bible in a positive light. They may have progressed well beyond friendship. They were likely homosexual affairs, although not necessarily sexually active relationships:

• Ruth 1:16, 2:10–11 between Ruth and Naomi;
• 1 Samuel 18:1–4, 1 Samuel 20:41–2 and 2 Samuel 1:25–6 between David and Jonathan. (Some translations of the Bible distort the original Hebrew text, particularly of 1 Samuel 20.)

☐ It is the subject of endless debate whether St Paul's prohibition of at least some homosexual acts was:

• for the people in the vicinity of the Mediterranean during the first century CE, or
• for all people, forever.

One can argue that the ancient Israelites were surrounded by warlike tribes. Their fertility was very important if the group was to survive. The early Christian Church was also surrounded by enemies. Homosexuals tend to have few children; thus their presence would be met with opposition. At the end of the twentieth century, conditions are the exact opposite; we are threatened by our excessive fertility.

Appendices

Perhaps Paul's criticism of homosexuality is no longer valid, like his various prohibitions against women's behaviour.

B. Women in the New Testament

□ □ □

A. The Jesus Tradition

Teaching on Family and Single Life

Parents	– Mark 10:19, 7:9–13
Children	– Mark 9:33–7, 10:13–16
Widows	– Mark 12:38–40, 41–4
Marriage/Adultery	– Matthew 5:27–30; John 8:2–11
Divorce	– Matthew 5:31–2, 19:3–9; Luke 16:18
'Eunochs'/Single Life	– Matthew 19:10–12

Parables and Sayings
Parables

Obstinate widow	– Luke 18:1–8
Lost coin	– Luke 15:8–10
Leaven/dough	– Matthew 13:33; Luke 13:20–1
Wise and foolish virgins	– Matthew 25:1–13

116

Sayings

Queen of the South	– Matthew 12:42; Luke 11:31
Final separation	– Luke 17:34–5; Matthew 24:40–2
Hens/weeping	– Matthew 23:37–9; Luke 13:34–5
Daughters	– Luke 23:27–31

Help and Healing

Lucan anointing	– Luke 7:36–50
At the well	– John 4:7–42
Syrophoenician	– Mark 7:24–30; Matthew 15:21–8
Peter's mother-in-law	– Mark 1:29–31; Matthew 8:14–15; Luke 4:38–9
Cripple on Sabbath	– Luke 13:10–17* (in synagogue)
Jairus and the Jewess	– Mark 5:21–43; Matthew 9:18–26; Luke 8:40–56
Widow of Nain	– Luke 7:11–17

Key Women in Jesus' Life

Mother Mary	– Wedding feast, John 2:1–12; at the cross, John 19:25–7; other mentions: Mark 3:19–21, 31–5; Matthew 12:46–50; Luke 8:19–21; Mark 6:1–6; Matthew 13:53–8; Luke 4:16–30.
Mary and Martha	– Hosts or guests, Luke 10:38–42; confession and proclamation, John 11:1–44; anointing, Mark 14:3–9; Matthew 26:6–13 and John 12:1–8.

Women who followed
Jesus   – Luke 8:1–3; at the cross,
                           Mark 15:40–1; Matthew
                           27:55–6; Luke 23:49; John
                           19:25.
Mary Magdalene   – Matthew 27:56, 61; John
                           19:25, 20:1, 18; Luke 24:10;
                           Mark 16:9 (other possible
                           references too).

B. The Pauline Tradition

Women and the Physical Family

Marriage, divorce and the single life	– 1 Corinthians 7
Exclusive monogamy	– Romans 7:1–3
Holiness and honour	– 1 Thessalonians 4:3–8
Mixed marriage	– 2 Corinthians 6:14–7:1
Colossian *Oikos*	– Colossians 3:18–4:1
Ephesian *Oikos*	– Ephesians 5:21–33

Women and Faith

Rites and rights	– Galatians 3:28
Unveiled threat	– 1 Corinthians 11:2–16
Silence	– 1 Corinthians 14:33b–6

Paul and his Female Co-workers

Trouble	– Philippians 4:2–3
Greetings	– Romans 16:1–16
Behaviour in worship	– 1 Timothy 2:8–15
Character of deaconess	– 1 Timothy 3:11

C. Birth, Resurrection and Acts

Birth	– see early chapters of Matthew and Luke; Elizabeth, Mary and Anna
Resurrection	– see concluding chapters of all 4 Gospels

Acts

Ananias and Sapphira	– 5:1–11
Drusilla and Bernice	– 25:13, 23, 26:30
Prominent women	– 17:4, 12
Mary/widow and Rhoda	– 12:12–17
Lydia	– 16:12–15, 23–40
Tabitha, deaconess	– 9:32–42 (6:1–7)
Prophets	– 21:9, 11:28, 21:10–11
Teachers	– 18:1–3, 24–6

(Adapted from Ben Witherington, *Women and the Genesis of Christianity* (Cambridge, CUP), 1990.)

---

* *Acts* has examples of 'parallelism', coupling male and female workers together. Sometimes the woman is mentioned first: e.g. Priscilla and Aquila.

C. Hymn to Wisdom

❐ ❐ ❐

1 My soul yearns for wisdom:
   and beyond all else my heart longs for her.
2 She has walked through the depths of the abyss:
   she has measured its boundaries;

3 For she was there from the beginning:
   and apart from her not one thing came to be.
4 She played before creation, when the world was made:
   and in her hands are all things held together.

5 She has danced upon the face of the deep:
   and all that hath breath is instinct with her life.
6 The mystery of creation is in her grasp:
   yet she delights to expound her ways.

7 So she abandons those who are wise in their
      own sight:
   but with all who are ready to receive her
   she makes her home.
8 For her delight is in the truth:
   and she takes no pleasure in deceitful ways;

9 Her integrity is more to be desired than comfort:
   and her discernment is more precious than security.
10 In her alone is the life of humanity:
   therefore while I live I will search her out;
11 For whoever is fed by wisdom will never hunger:
   and all who drink from her will never thirst again.

GLORIA
   (Adapted from Janet Morley, *All Desires Known*, SPCK, 1992)

D. Some Recommended Reading

Ashkenazy, N., *Eve's Journey: Feminine Images in Hebraic Literary Tradition*, Pennsylvania, University of Pennsylvania Press, 1986.

Avis, P., *Eros and the Sacred*, London, SPCK, 1989.

Borrowdale, A., *Distorted Images: Christian Attitudes to Women, Men and Sex*, London, SPCK, 1991.

Boswell, J., *Christianity, Social Tolerance and Homosexuality*, Chicago, University Press, 1980.

Brash, A., *Facing Our Differences*, London, Council for Churches in Britain and Ireland, 1996.

Bynum, C., *Fragmentation and Redemption: Essays on Gender and the Human Body in Medieval Religion*, New York, Zone Books, 1992.

Byrne, L., Lonsdale, D. and Sheldrake, P., *The Way: Contemporary Christian Spirituality – Sexuality and Spirituality*, London, The Way Publications, vol. 28, no. 3., July 1988.

Cooper-White, P., *The Cry of Tamar: Violence Against Women and the Church's Response*, Minneapolis, Fortress Press, 1995.

Countryman, W., *Dirt, Greed and Sex*, London, SCM, 1989.

The Truth About Love, London, SPCK/Triangle, 1993.

Dare, C. and Pincus, L., *Secrets in the Family*, London, Faber & Faber, 1978.

Douglas, M., *Purity and Danger: An Analysis of the Concept of Pollution and Taboo*, New York, Pantheon Books, 1966.

Dowell, S. and Hurcombe, L., *Dispossessed Daughters of Eve*, London, SPCK, 1981.

Fiorenza, E., *In Memory of Her*, London, SCM, 1983.

Foucault, M., *Madness and Civilisation*, New York, Random House, 1965.

The History of Sexuality, Volume 1, New York, Random House, 1978.

Furlong, M. (ed.), *Mirror to the Church*, London, SPCK, 1988.

Gill, S., *Women and the Church of England*, London, SPCK, 1994.

Grey, M., *The Wisdom of Fools*, London, SPCK, 1991.

Heine, S., *Women and Early Christianity*, London, SCM, 1986.

Heyward, C., *Touching Our Strength: The Erotic as Power and the Love of God*, San Francisco, Harper & Row, 1989.

Holloway, R. (ed.), *Who Needs Feminism?* London, SPCK, 1991.

Horner, T., *Homosexuality in Biblical Times*, Philadelphia, Westminster, 1978.

Hunt, M., *Fierce Tenderness: A Feminist Theology of Friendship*, New York, Crossroad, 1991.

Jantzen, G., *Julian of Norwich*, London, SPCK, 1987.

Power, Gender and Christian Mysticism, Cambridge, CUP, 1995.

Jones, L., *Embodying Forgiveness*, Grand Rapids, Eerdmans, 1995.

Keller, C., *From a Broken Web*, Boston, Beacon Press, 1986.

Kennedy, H., *Eve Was Framed*, London, Chatto & Windus, 1990.

Mackey, J., *Power and Christian Ethics*, Cambridge, CUP, 1994.

Mickley, R., *Christian Sexuality: A Reflection on Being*

Christian and Sexual, Los Angeles, Universal Fellowship Press, 1976.

Miles, M., *Carnal Knowing*, Boston, Beacon Press, 1989.

Moore, S., *Let This Mind Be in You: The Quest for Identity Through Oedipus to Christ*, London, DLT, 1985.

The Inner Loneliness, London, DLT, 1982.

Morley, J., *All Desires Known* (revised edition), 1994.

Celebrating Women, London, SPCK, 1995.

Murray, T. and McClure, M., *Moral Panic: Exposing the Religious Right's Agenda on Sexuality*, London, Cassell, 1995.

Nelson, B. and Longfellow, P., *Sexuality and the Sacred: Sources for Theological Reflection*, London, Mowbray, 1994.

Nelson, J., *Embodiment: An Approach to Sexuality and Christian Theology*, Augsburg, Fortress, 1978.

Nicholson, R., *God in Aids? A Theological Enquiry*, London, SCM, 1995.

Oraison, M., *The Homosexual Question*, New York, Harper & Row, 1977.

Oz, A., *Where the Jackals Howl*, New York, Harcourt Brace Jovanovich, 1981.

Pittenger, N., *Gay Lifestyles: A Christian Interpretation of Homosexuality and the Homosexual*, Los Angeles, Universal Fellowship Press, 1977.

Pryce, M., *Finding a Voice*, London, SCM, 1996.

Rose, G., *Love's Work*, London, Chatto & Windus, 1995.

Ruether, R. R., *Sexism and God-Talk*, London, SCM, 1983.

Russell, L. and Shannon Clarkson, J., *Dictionary of Feminist Theologies*, London, Mowbray, 1996.

Sanderson, T., *Mediawatch*, London, Cassell, 1995.

Scroggs, R., *The New Testament and Homosexuality*, Philadelphia, Fortress Press, 1983.

Spong, J., *Living in Sin?* New York, Harper & Row, 1988.

Storkey, E., *What's Right With Feminism?* London, SPCK, 1985.

Stuart, E., *Daring to Speak Love's Name*, London, Hamish Hamilton, 1992.

Just Good Friends: Towards a Lesbian and Gay Theology of Relationships, London, Cassell, 1995.

Spitting at Dragons: Towards a Feminist Theology of Sainthood, London, Mowbray, 1996.

Thatcher, A. & Stuart, E., *Sexuality and Gender*, Gracewing/Fowler-Wright, 1996.

People of Passion: What the Churches Teach About Sex, London, Mowbray, 1997.

Trible, P., *God and the Rhetoric of Sexuality*, Philadelphia, Fortress Press, 1978.

Turner, P., *Sex, Money and Power*, Boston, Cowley, 1985.

Vasey, M., *Strangers and Friends: A New Exploration of Homosexuality and the Bible*, London, Hodder & Stoughton, 1995.

Walton, H., 'Theology of Desire', *Theology and Sexuality*, no. 1, Sept. 1994.

Webster, A., *Found Wanting: Women, Sexuality and Christianity*, London, Cassell, 1995.

Weeks, J., *Sex, Politics and Society: The Regulation of Sexuality Since 1800* (2nd edition), London, Longman, 1989.

Williams, R., *The Body's Grace*, London, LGCM, 1989.

Witherington, B., *Women and the Genesis of Christianity*, Cambridge, CUP, 1990.

Woods, R., *Another Kind of Love: Homosexuality and Spirituality*, Garden City, NY, Doubleday, 1978.

World-Wide-Web Sites: For specific subjects try *http://www.god.co.uk*, or *The Internet and World Wide Web*, ed. A.J. Kennedy, London, Rough Guides, 1995.

E. Short Index

□ □ □